The Kingdom Algorithm

How to Apply the Bible to Your Life

Books by Gary T. Cage

The Holy Spirit, A Sourcebook with Commentary

Clothed With Power, A Brief Study of the Indwelling of the Holy Spirit

The Woodsman, A Novel

Also Related

Truth, Faith, and Liberty,
A Collection of Essays Honoring Gary T. Cage

Order from:
Charlotte House Publishers
P.O. Box 50147
Reno, NV 89513-0147

gary.cage@gmail.com

The Kingdom Algorithm
How to Apply the Bible to Your Life

By Gary T. Cage
with Bill Orr

Charlotte House Publishers
Reno, Nevada

Charlotte House Publishers
P. O. Box 50147
Reno, NV 89513-0147

The Kingdom Algorithm, How To Apply the Bible To Your Life
By Gary T. Cage with Bill Orr
Copyright 2014 Charlotte House Publishers
ISBN: 0-9654828-4-7

Algorithm: a procedure for solving a mathematical problem (as of finding the greatest common divisor) in a finite number of steps that frequently involves repetition of an operation; broadly: a step-by-step procedure for solving a problem or accomplishing some end especially by a computer.

Table of Contents

Foreword

Behavioral psychologists have focused on the environment as a significant factor in the control of human behavior, such as the writing of a book. The book in your hands will most likely challenge some very old and widely accepted ideas. But, this book didn't occur in a vacuum. It, and others like it, came out of a rich, intellectual environment that is not often found in modern religious circles of serious and committed Christians. This environment has been propaedeutic to this book and the many other positive outcomes we have enjoyed over the years at the Comstock Chapel.

Some 30 years ago in a series of strange events, I stumbled across Professor Gary Cage one Sunday morning in a small, conservative church in Reno. It was not what I had expected. I had attended once before under pressure from a friend and had no intention of returning, but the atmosphere of openness, warmth and an apparently serious search for truth surprised me and enticed my interest.

My personal journey, after having been asked to leave a church for teaching what I thought the Bible clearly taught, had left me cynical, out of the ministry, and therefore, very doubtful that an honest search for the truth would ever be found in an organized church. After some time in this titillating environment of new openness and many long discussions on numerous topics, one day Gary asked me, "So Bob, what are we going to do with the Bible?" This question was asked seriously, in a way that most Christians, and I myself from a previous time, could not even have allowed. But, there it was. I was pleasantly stunned. So, everything really was open to question! There was no immediate response, but we both knew this question really needed to be answered. After many conversations and some refinement the issue became, the topic of this book, namely, how consistently to apply the New Testament to our lives today.

The open discussion and question-stimulating atmosphere was evident in several Sunday afternoon classes over the years. The Holy Spirit study led to an enormously important book. The Christian Evidence study led to an unpublished collection of documents for repeated classes and then an online class hosted on the Internet. There were classes on Ancient Biblical History, the Apocrypha, the Pseudepigrapha and other Inter-Testamental literature, the Age of the Universe, Sexuality, Logical Thinking, Communication, and many other topics. Bill Orr, when he isn't working on the Algorithm, has maintained a long-standing debate with a group of us over whether God is necessarily logical or created logic as a part of the Universe. It is not uncommon to hear constructive arguments and debates in dyads or larger groups on the nature of God, theology, various doctrines or other philosophical issues. It is like what a university used to be.

A few years ago, in a High School Bible class I was teaching, we asked the students to develop a consistent way to use the New Testament in their lives. They read through the entire New Testament looking for commands and promises that would apply to all people for all times. We asked the students to develop a logical method to decide which passages would apply universally. They had some difficulty laying out the principles, but found many passages they agreed upon as universal. We dubbed these as Purple Letter passages. One of the young men was convinced that we could make a lot of money if we published the Purple Letter Edition. This process of learning led to many spirited discussions among the teenagers, which sometimes spread to their parents, and others in the church. While our results were unsophisticated and never published (sorry Mat), the effort and struggles were instructive to both the students and the teacher.

Recently, I was approached by a rather conservative and very sincere Christian brother who asked, "Do I fit in here?" The "here" he was concerned about was that environment, lauded above, which supports "challenging very old ideas." I was able to respond quickly. "Yes, you fit in here and are important as a brother for your input and ideas." Not just old ideas, but all ideas and especially new ones, need to be challenged continuously, if we are truly in pursuit of the truth. In fact, our carefully constructed mission statement, written many years ago, answers this question more broadly, and has helped create this open and accepting environment.

"We, the family of God, at Comstock Chapel, commit ourselves to the open pursuit of the Truth of the Gospel; present that Truth to others in Love; support and build up one another in all matters of Christian citizenship-that we might expand and strengthen the Kingdom of God."

The environment at Comstock Chapel includes a broad assortment of people, men and women, young and older, conservative, liberal and libertarian, some blue and some white collars, and a few with no collar at all. While all of these people are important contributors, none of this would have occurred without the servant-hearted leadership of Dr. Gary Cage. Prolonged contact with this man has deeply affected my thinking, my life, and especially my life in the Kingdom.

So, I heartily encourage you to read this book with an open mind. Give it a serious look. Expect some challenges to what you have believed to be true. Carefully construct your objections and opinions and present them to the author. After all, these new ideas, like all the old ones, need to be continuously challenged in an honest pursuit of the truth.

Dr. Bob Hemenway
Agape Psychological Services
April 2014

Preface

Followers of Christ, we have a problem! The problem, simply put, is this: we all use different techniques for interpreting and applying scripture. Everyone uses a system with regard to applying the Bible to his life, and those different systems make a huge difference in our lives. Many times the system a disciple uses is not even fully understood by the reader that is using it. We usually use a system because it is traditional, familiar and comfortable, but if and when the system fails to make sense, we tend to ignore the little inconsistencies and get on with living for God.

Have you ever asked yourself how is it that there are so many hugely differing systems of belief and sets of practices within Christianity? How did we get here? Also, if we all are using different systems to interpret scripture, what is it that would make any one of these systems any better than any other? Could we all at least agree that our methodology needs to be consistent? If any system does not or cannot pass the test of basic consistency, then that should be a warning sign that the system is faulty. You see, although consistency does not prove that a system is right, any inconsistency does prove that the system is wrong. This book is an effort to lay out systematically the ideas of a kingdom algorithm, which we believe to be a truly consistent method for reading the Bible and applying biblical principles to our lives.

Bill Orr's Story

When I was going to Bible College in Nebraska, I had some nagging questions. Among those questions was the one that we are addressing in this book. At the time, I decided that the question itself was not a good question partly because it was not the sort of thing that a good Christian boy would contemplate, much less bring up, and partly because I accepted as true some overarching beliefs that eliminated this nagging question from my radar. The thinking was like this: If I accepted (and I did) the Bible as the inerrant and inspired word of God sent to all mankind for all times, then all that I needed to do in the area of interpretation was to figure out what that Bible said, believe it, and do it.

Simple; right? As it turns out, it was not nearly as simple as I had originally thought. The thing is, the questions didn't stop there, and the answers kept getting more and more convoluted the deeper I went into the effort to understand the issue. Questions like, "Do you believe in plenary inspiration (the idea that the very words on the page were inspired), or do you think that it was the writers who were inspired?" Or, "If these words are for all people for all time, can these words actually mean something different to one generation than they mean to another?" Or, "Why do we spend so much time trying to figure out what the original writer said and meant when he was talking to his original audience when we are just going to say that the Bible says it directly to me?"

Another equally disturbing problem was the inconsistency of our treatment of the Bible. And it seemed that we never tried to deal with that inconsistency. For example, in my fellowship, the argument in favor of the necessity of baptism was supported by the reasoning that "The Bible says to do it, and therefore we are taking away from the word of God if we ignore the Bible teaching on the subject," while at the same time saying that "Other teachings in the Bible are obviously not meant to be followed by us, because these instructions were meant only for the people of that day."

A lot of these questions came much later, after I had graduated college and moved on. As is often the case, I changed my beliefs about some of these teachings later in life and began down a road that has been at times exhilarating, and at times terrifying. As I began reworking my belief system in an effort to find the truth, I eventually ended up back at the following quandary: if the writings in the Bible were not written to me, and if a large portion of the New Testament is a compilation of letters, then that means we are essentially reading other people's mail. How then do I know which things I ought to follow and do, and how do I know which things were never were intended for me to follow today? I was fortunate enough to fall in with a group of Christian men that, although they did not have all the answers, were willing and even enjoyed seeking the truth in matters such as this. The beauty of this group of men is that they are the most loving and honest men you could ever want to meet, but they don't hold back either. Come to find out, this question had been bothering some of these people too. Gary Cage said that this question had been on his mind for years. We would have discussions about this topic for hours on end, and even read books that added to the discussion. One of the men, Dr. Bob Hemenway, even tried to get to the bottom of this question by working on a purple letter edition of the Bible, in which everything that was intended as obligatory for all Christ followers, for all time, would be in purple letters – much like the red letter editions, in which all Jesus' words are in red. The effort failed in becoming a finished product, but was very helpful in the long run because of all the interest and discussion that it stirred up.

The importance of this topic and the idea that we didn't have an answer to it really bothered me. How could we stand there and tell ourselves, or anyone else for that matter, what they ought to be doing as based on the Biblical teaching when we had no idea how rightly to figure out in a consistent manner exactly which things apply to us today and which do not? This drove me on, even to the point that I really began to irritate people, because I was a bit obsessed with the question and the importance of finding an answer.

One time on a drive up to and back from a men's retreat, I had the time to discuss the topic with my brother-in-law, Ty Jones. He is one of the most intelligent and talented people I know, and so I was hopeful that he just might be able to solve my dilemma in the car ride. Unfortunately, he wasn't, but he did make a huge contribution to the effort.

Ty is a computer engineer, and as he listened to me talking about the problem and the many efforts toward a solution, he told me that he knew what we needed. "What you are looking for is an algorithm," he said. He went on to discuss how algorithms are used in computing and in math, and thus the pursuit of "the Algorithm," or a consistent method for applying the New Testament, began.

There were many, many attempts to find this consistent method, and many, many ideas that proved faulty in the end. I still have a few different ideas that I penned out and brought to this group of men to see if we could find the holes in the approach, and we always did. It was a couple years later that Gary Gage had an idea. We ought just to go through the New Testament, he suggested, and find all the passages that we thought were for all time, and then maybe a system would appear to us along the way. This is the method used in the sciences, he added.

I have to admit that I was a bit skeptical about this approach at first. I had already tried a similar approach and had made little progress. I thought that we needed to come up with the system first, and then when we read the text, it would make sense, and not the other way around. I was open to the idea, though, because we had made no real progress to date, other than to know that what we were doing was not the right way to do it. So we started reading, and to my surprise, and Gary's too, we both separately came to the same conclusion: that the kingdom of heaven or the kingdom of God was the answer that we had been looking for. We have tried to "sink our own ship," in a manner of speaking, with this new system, and yet it has stood the test. After some fine-tuning and study, we have the algorithm described in this book.

Gary Cage's Story

The following true story from a close and trusted friend of mine illustrates how a system of interpretation influences behavior and religious beliefs:

> The deacon had a scolding look on his face as he stood there holding in his hand my niece's baby bottle. He said, "This is not the scriptural use of the refrigerator!" I apologetically retrieved the bottle of milk and respectfully explained that my sister had not meant any harm. It was the middle of the summer with over 100-

degree temperatures. My sister had placed the bottle in the refrigerator so the contents would not spoil. At the time, the thought had never occurred to us that this action might be perceived as sinful, but in retrospect, seeing the milk bottle in the deacon's hand reminds me of the many sermons I had heard throughout my life regarding the appropriate use of items which had been purchased by the church treasury (such as the refrigerator).

As ridiculous as this story may sound, we need to realize that many different Christian groups have reached startlingly different conclusions as to what the Bible means and how to apply it. The previous story occurred in a church that operated on a hermeneutical principle that declared biblical silence prohibitive; that is, unless the scriptures specifically allow for an action, it is sinful. This type of reasoning is not uncommon. Many differing religions today have similar methods of interpretation that are seemingly "sound doctrine" at first glance but when played out in real life are bordering on, if not immersed in, the absurd. Examples such as this can be found in all the different religious groups. But in this particular church on the occasion of this story, the deacon was reminding these women of the venerable principle that a refrigerator which had been bought with church money could be used only for keeping the elements of the Lord's Supper – certainly not for anything so mundane as cooling an infant's milk.

I was raised in the church. I love the church. I love the Bible. I love God. All of this so much so, in fact, that I have dedicated my whole life to the promotion of the knowledge of God in the world. I went to Christian colleges and trained to be a minister, which is what I have been, besides being an instructor in the local college system, for forty years. In my fourth year of college I rose at 5:00 most mornings of the school year to make a list of all of the commandments of the New Testament, in an effort to systematize a complete list of commandments for Christians. I can today smile at the naiveté of that time, but it was a sincere effort on my part to have a clear idea of what I was to do in the kingdom. However, even then I noticed that many of the commandments did not seem to have any application to me. Over the years, not only have I continued to struggle with the inconsistency of the practice of applying some biblical texts while not applying others, but many others, including some of my closest colleagues in the ministry, have expressed the same bewilderment.

Then I ran into Bill Orr. The brother is relentless. I worked out systems to try to answer the question he was raising, but there were always flaws. For fourteen months in 2004 and 2005, we worked side by side in the physical construction of a church plant. The discussion of the issue of how consistently to apply the Bible to our lives went on continuously. I can still picture in my mind one day in particular, while we were completing the irrigation system, that, shovels in hand, we tried one more attempt at a solution – only to fail. I owe Bill a great deal for neither giving up nor settling for inconsistency.

The Plan of This Book

We, the authors, have come to realize that many churches, even in the same general fellowship, come to different conclusions regarding proper godly behavior. It has become clear to us that there is a problem. In the beginning, we couldn't put our finger on the exact root of the matter, however it appeared that we were not the only ones chafing under this condition. Even some of the great leaders in our movement had differed among themselves over this. There was a lot of debate about how church issues were to be approached, issues such as church attendance, musical instruments in the worship service, whether or not supporting missionary work was a scriptural use of church funds, whether or not a church building can have a kitchen in it, (and this is only addressing the disagreements within just one sector of our fellowship), and on and on. The point is that there are many strong opinions on these and many other topics, but the real problem seems to lie beneath (as it usually does), at the very foundation of the principles that are being taught. We as Christians tend to get embroiled in debates yet overlook the real issues. Few of us are ready to recognize that the very system that we are using to interpret the Bible is flawed. Without this realization, the debates continue interminably. When faced with inconsistency in our teaching, we often try desperately to fix the problem, but at the wrong level. It's much like treating the symptom, rather than the disease.

The position that was taken regarding "the scriptural use of the refrigerator" has many inherent problems. To start with, how could one use the hermeneutical principle declaring that biblical silence is prohibitive (that is, unless the scriptures specifically allow for an action, it is sinful) to back up this contention, when if used consistently, this very hermeneutic would actually mandate that there be no refrigerator to begin with? Even more problematic is the actual fact that this hermeneutic often has superseded the "Second Greatest Commandment" by making it more important that one maintain the proper "scriptural use of a refrigerator" than that one love his Christian sister.

Perhaps as you read the refrigerator story, you were thinking you could top it with a personal story from your own history. We would not be surprised to find that many Christians had similar stories. But the beauty in this story is that when a hermeneutic, taken to its logical conclusion, produces an outlandish result, it is a great big red flag that the foundational hermeneutic needs to be critiqued. This book is based on the premise that many Christians have been bewildered by the apparent inconsistent use of the Bible in churches and in Christians' lives. In fact, as we shall discuss later, there has been a raft of books recently which have exposed a similar concern in the minds of many other God loving people.

Reading the Bible and understanding what it says is one thing, but applying the teachings to our lives is another. In the pages that follow, we would like to discuss how applying biblical teachings has become something of a problem for many people, how sometimes people can find remarkably strange applications in the Bible, how followers of Christ can sometimes be flagrantly inconsistent in their use of the Bible, and how this has created an image problem for Christianity in our culture.

We, the authors, have struggled with this question for many years. We sincerely want to be what God wants us to be, and we respect the Bible as a record of God's revelation of His mind to human beings over the centuries. We also respect the many people who have taken the Bible seriously, wanting to be correct in their obedience to God. Nothing of what we say in the following pages is meant to ridicule these people. Anybody who has high regard for God and His message deserves and has earned our respect. Certainly, such an attitude is much better than a flippant disregard for God's will. However, it has become patently obvious to us that sincere Christians apply the principles of the scriptures, not only wildly differently from each other, but also even inconsistently in their own lives.

This book, then, is not about interpreting scripture but rather about how to apply the scriptures to our lives as followers of Christ in a consistent manner. Even after one has made his or her best effort to determine what the sentences and paragraphs mean in a biblical text, there is still the problem of knowing whether and how that passage applies to one's life. For example, one might read the story of David and Goliath and understand the story, but what still remains are the original two questions: does this text apply to my life, and if so, how does it apply?

As we said above, we have debated this issue for years among ourselves. We have talked about the matter to a great number of people. We have read books on the subject. Until recently we have been frustrated and disappointed. However, we think we have found an answer. We call it The Kingdom Algorithm, and here it is. We think we should read the Bible for the story of the kingdom of God, a story which culminates in the work of Jesus Christ. Whatever, then, one finds to be inextricably connected to the kingdom of God (or the kingdom of heaven or the kingdom of Christ) is what is binding on all followers of Christ for all times, in all places and in all cultures. By that we mean that whatever is set forth in the Bible as necessary to citizenship in the kingdom is, according to our algorithm, incumbent on all Christians for all time. Otherwise, those other things in the Bible, though highly illustrative of God's nature and will, are not incumbent. So, we'll be looking for explicit statements in the Bible on the kingdom of God.

In the pages that follow, we will, in Chapter 1, make the problem clearer, giving some examples. In Chapter 2, we will set out some responses to this problem we have encountered over the years. However, we have found those responses either unhelpful or unsuccessful. Chapter 3 starts the hard work of setting out and defending The Kingdom Algorithm. There we will take pains to examine the four gospels in order to find descriptions of the kingdom of God. Our argument will be that the kingdom is of such a nature as to yield itself to being an algorithm for sifting the New Testament for what is intended for all Christians for all times. Chapter 4 will continue with the four gospels, only this time the concern will be to isolate the conditions necessary to citizenship in God's kingdom. There will be some effort made at summarizing those conditions, but a fuller account of them will be held off until a later chapter. Then Chapter 5 will cover the rest of the New Testament. Since one of the best ways to see what the aims of Jesus were is to see what his immediate followers did, we will look at the kingdom language of Acts, Paul's writings, the Book of Revelation and the rest. Now, as we shall see, the kingdom can be discussed in the New Testament even when the word "kingdom" isn't used; there are other terms for it. Chapter 6 deals with those passages. Then, in Chapter 7, we will run a test. One could legitimately argue that maybe salvation is just as central to the New Testament as is the kingdom, if not more so, so we will compile salvation passages to compare the conditions for attaining salvation to the conditions for citizenship in the kingdom. We think we pass the test. That brings us to Chapter 8, where we summarize our findings and describe the universal citizen of the kingdom of God, that is, we set out in detail what is required of all Christ followers in all times, places and cultures. We recognize that, for some, the things we are going to say are new and different and that this algorithm will raise a lot of questions. Chapter 9 lists some possible objections that might be brought against our algorithm, and we address all of those before we conclude with what the algorithm of the kingdom will mean in the lives of modern Christians who are reading and applying the Bible to their lives today.

Acknowledgements

We would like to thank Patty Orr for so much support in so many ways. She played a big role in our thinking, being willing to offer criticisms and suggestions, as well as much encouragement. Dr. Bob Hemenway has for many years been a part of the conversation which eventuated in this book. He once conceived of a "Purple-Letter Edition" of the Bible, in which those verses in the Bible which can be taken off the page and applied directly to our lives would be printed with purple ink. He has also challenged much of our thinking along the way. We thank Caleb Cage, a writer himself, for his encouragement and his commitment to editing and publishing this work. And many thanks to those lovely disciples of Jesus who meet at the Comstock Chapel in Reno, Nevada, for supporting an atmosphere that encourages thinking.

1 What is the Problem?

In I Timothy 2.8-15 we read,

> I want men everywhere to pray. They should lift up holy hands as they pray. They should not be angry or argue. Christian women should not be dressed in the kind of clothes and their hair should not be combed in a way that will make people look at them. They should not wear much gold or pearls or clothes that cost much money. Instead of these things, Christian women should be known for doing good things and living good lives.

> Women should be quiet when they learn. They should listen to what men have to say. I never let women teach men or be leaders over men. They should be quiet. Adam was made first, then Eve. Adam was not fooled by Satan; it was the woman who was fooled and sinned. But women will be saved through the giving of birth to children if they keep on in faith and live loving and holy lives.

Historically this passage has been relied upon by some Bible readers to support the view that women should not have a publicly prominent role in the assembly. This has been interpreted this way by many different people that are associated with different groups, but they share the core belief that women should not preside in the assembly. However, in this same passage that they have used to support this interpretation there is a command that men should pray lifting up holy hands. Although some churches make that a requirement, many churches see it as optional. Some churches disregard it all together. This is the problem of this book. Why do Bible readers choose to impose one commandment and disregard another, sometimes when both commandments can be found in the same paragraph?

A prominent mantra in evangelical Christianity is that the Bible is the word of God. And inasmuch as it is the word of God, the follower of Christ has only to read the Bible and do what it says. By this it is meant that no sophisticated hermeneutical theory is required for reading and obeying the Bible. That is, one needs no philosophical approach to the Bible; he has only to pick it up and read the commandments of God and obey them. One often even hears it said, "I just read the Bible, believe what it says and then do it; it's simple." In this book we are arguing that people do indeed sometimes have philosophical approaches to the text which determine which verses they see as commandments and which ones they ignore. We are arguing that all readers of the Bible have some sort of hermeneutical system, though it is almost always unacknowledged, and worse, it is usually inconsistent.

In Matthew 19.16-30 (a passage to which we shall turn several times in this book), a rich young man accosts Jesus with the question of what he must do to inherit eternal life. It must be acknowledged that this is a very important question. In the case of Jesus' response, the young man was told to go and sell all that he had, give it to the poor, and then come and follow Jesus. Very seldom, at least in America, is this commandment followed to the letter. In the first few chapters of the Book of Acts the early Christians were enjoined to sell their goods and pool their money for purposes of supporting financially those believers who were in need. Even though believers today often give of their means to help the unfortunate, seldom do we follow the example of the early church to the extent of this example. What is the principle of interpretation and application of biblical passages that followers of Christ are using today when they decide to help other people financially?

Some Christians point to passages like Romans 10:9 that say that if you believe God raised Jesus from the dead you will be saved, while ignoring similar passages like Acts 2:38, which teach that one must be baptized to be saved. Then there are those who would point to passages on baptism insisting on baptism as part of the salvation process, while at the same time passing over passages on tongue speaking as inapplicable to Christians today. Our question is: why some passages and not others?

In the New Testament books of 1 Timothy and Titus, Paul commanded these young namesakes to establish in their churches committees of leaders which were variously styled "elders" "bishops" or "presbyters". One has only to course through the history of Christianity to see that churches have seldom stayed with this original design. In the second century, a distinction was made between the head elder, the bishop, and the rest of the elders. Throughout the centuries we have seen the rise of abbots, cardinals, popes, and patriarchs. In modern American Christianity, many progressive churches are modeled after the structure of General Motors, with a senior pastor, assistant pastors, and board of elders, very much like the CEO, vice presidents, and directors of a typical American corporation. It is not our intent to say at this point which, if any, of these approaches are right; we are asking the question only, by what principle are decisions of styles of leadership made?

Several years ago at a religious conference, a speaker was tasked with discussing the issue of the homosexual lifestyle and its interface with biblical teaching. At the beginning of his third installment, he brought up the issue of the role of women in the church. For several minutes he spoke about 1 Corinthians 14 and how Paul enjoined the women in Corinth to be silent in the assembly. It appeared to all who were there that the conference speaker had forgotten his topic, but he knew very well what he was doing. After discussing the role of women for a few minutes, he asked the questions, should we apply these teachings of 1 Corinthians to our churches today? Next, he considered the objection that some might make, that Paul was addressing a situation that applied to Christians in the first century but would not necessarily apply to us today (the "that was then, but this is now" argument). He then added that he had not forgotten his topic. He knew his topic was homosexuality and the Bible. He said, however, that he had brought up the issue of the role of women because someone might very well use this same argument and say, "That was then, but this is now". In other words, the speaker argued, some people would apply Biblical statements about homosexuality to the church today, while at the same time insisting that the statements about women do not apply, but never set out the principle as to why that is the case. That exactly is the question of this book: what is the principle that we use to decide which biblical passages apply to us today and which do not?

In the authors' own fellowship there has been plenty of this inconsistency--and to spare. Our fellowship, which among other names, has been known as the Restoration Movement, was begun by a group of heady optimists who sought to engender the greatest possible amount of unity among Christian believers as the freedom of this new land of the United States of America would allow. The result has been a sad irony, one of splitting, dissension and bitterness. Here are some of the principles of the Restoration Movement as it can be found today throughout the world. Some would argue that the silence of the scriptures is prohibitive, that is, that if a behavior cannot be found as an approved behavior in the Bible, then it is sinful. This led to a really bizarre hermeneutic in which it was taught that Christians could do only those things which are established by a New Testament command, example or some action that could be shown to be implied by "necessary inference" (the last concept forming a catchall category for whatever behaviors the user thought acceptable). Others in the movement saw the Bible functioning as the Constitution did at the formation of our country. This led to a kind of formal patternism, whereby Christians were enjoined to recreate the very patterns of worship and practice as found in the New Testament. And lastly, there has been in our movement an ahistorical reading of the biblical texts, that is, the texts are read through the lens of some agenda, such as a legalistic agenda, or a doctrinal one, rather than a reading of the texts for what they really are, that is, tracts, letters or inspirational writings, written for the concerns of the original recipients. There has been in our own movement much bemoaning of the stalemate to which all of this has led. However, to our knowledge no clear program for solving this problem has been set forth. One writer in our tradition even said that, after seeing how inconsistently the Bible had been applied in his particular fellowship, he had come to the conclusion that the one he had received by tradition could not the correct one.[1]

However, lest someone think that this is an isolated phenomenon, the problem has surfaced everywhere. A. J. Jacobs, in his book *A Year of Living Biblically,* tells how, as a Jew, he set out to live, just a year, according to the precepts of the Old Testament, but found himself unable to do so. For example, he points to the commandment to stone homosexuals. Are faithful Jews supposed to do that today?[2]

But probably one of the more broadly accessible attempts at dealing with this problem is Scot McKnight's *The Blue Parakeet.* He tells the amusing story of watching birds around his bird feeder at his home in the Great Lakes Region. He knew the various species indigenous to his area, so when one day he saw a blue parakeet in his yard, it took him by surprise. Upon reflection, he concluded that the parakeet was someone's pet which had escaped his cage. McKnight then calls upon his readers to think of "blue parakeet passages" in the Bible, that is, passages which, when we encounter them, make us stop and ask the question, "Are these passages for us today or not?" Examples provided by McKnight include passages on subjects like the Sabbath, tithing, foot washing, charismatic gifts, evolution, Calvinism and participation in war. According to McKnight, Christians say they believe the Bible to be the word of God, they say they believe everything the Bible says, and they say they are committed to doing everything it teaches. But they don't; none of them does. They pick and choose from among the teachings, apparently regarding some of these teachings as blue parakeets. In his words, "The discoveries and disturbances converged into one big question: How, then, are we to live out the Bible today?"[3] That's our question, too.

McKnight is not talking about the well-known problem of people picking and choosing among those teachings on the basis of convenience, such as a disciple's choosing to participate in a drunken party

---

1 Todd Deaver, *Facing Our Failure, The Fellowship Dilemma in Conservative Churches of Christ,* Oliver Springs, TN, 2008, p. 14.

2 A.J. Jacobs, *The Year of Living Biblically: One Man's Humble Quest to Follow the Bible as Literally as Possible,* New York: Simon and Schuster, 2008, pp. 263-267.

3 Scot McKnight, *The Blue Parakeet, Rethinking How to Read Your Bible,* Grand Rapids: Zondervan, 2008, p. 17.

even though he knows it's sinful. He's talking about well-intentioned disciples who live exemplary lives but simply ignore certain teachings in the Bible. They don't seem interested in questions about these teachings. Or they respond to questions by saying that it's the principle that matters and not the actual action commanded in the text. Or they reply that that was then and this is now. And certainly, the questions about ignored passages nearly always scare people – on both sides of every issue. McKnight's best example centers on Leviticus 19, which has commandments about gleaning, prohibiting planting a field with two different types of seeds and about how not to trim one's beard. But in the middle of the chapter, verse 18, there is the command to love one's neighbor as oneself, a commandment made central by Jesus himself. Bible readers today almost universally ignore all of the commandments in Leviticus 19, while emphasizing verse 18. In McKnight's word, they see the other verses as blue parakeets.[4]

McKnight offers his solution in three words: story, listening and discernment.[5] By story he suggests that we disciples need to know the story of the Bible in order to get to know God by knowing how God crafted a grand narrative out of many smaller narratives. By listening he emphasizes the importance of an obedient heart on the part of the Bible reader; the importance of the story is that the listener enters into a relationship with God. And by discernment he means that we already have in our practice of applying biblical principles formed patterns of discernment that guide us. In McKnight's words, "we don't follow Jesus literally, we do pick and choose what we want to apply to our lives today, and I want to know what methods, ideas, and principles are at work among us for picking what we pick and choosing what we choose".[6]

We are very sympathetic with McKnight's quandary, and we will have more to say about his views later, but he has done an excellent job of setting out the problem.

With all that we have said above, the point is that most people who would call themselves Christians today would insist that they use the Bible as their guide in personal living, in morals, and in church organization. However, we have found a conspicuous absence of a clear

---

4 *Ibid.*, pp. 115-120.

5 *Ibid.*, p. 37.

6 *Ibid.*, p.122.

hermeneutical principle that sets out definitively why certain practices should be maintained and others should not. The writers we have looked at above show that this is not a new question, nor is it an isolated question. People over a wide range have noticed that there is something wrong with our general use of the Bible. Furthermore, even when a principle is sometimes enunciated as to how to use the Bible in our modern lives, that principle is seldom, if ever consistently applied.

Now, someone might complain at this point that we are making the matter far more complicated than it needs to be. We are very sympathetic with that complaint, and we want to make the following point eminently clear: anybody can read his Bible, sincerely follow Jesus and go to be with God eternally without a self-conscious awareness of any certain principle of hermeneutics. Now, it is important to repeat ourselves: anybody can read his Bible, sincerely follow Jesus and go to be with God eternally without a self-conscious awareness of any certain principle of hermeneutics. In fact, we think this point will be borne out in this book. And we are very concerned about snobbery, philosophical, theological or otherwise. There is no desire on our part to belittle anyone's sincere attempt to use the Bible to follow the Messiah, nor is there a disposition on our part to establish an elite society of biblical specialists. However, the question of this book presents us with a dilemma. On the one hand, we don't want to make Bible reading so sophisticated that people are discouraged from it. But on the other hand, we don't want to minimize the seriousness of the issue. All of us Christ followers should want to get it right, we should want to understand the Bible the best we can and we should want to draw from it those principles which God would have us draw and apply. There is also the prospect that we might either miss something truly important by using the wrong principles of biblical application or, worse, get some important biblical teaching wrong and then pass it on to others. But as can be seen from the discussion already, the question which we are taking up on this book has perplexed many. This book is an effort to deal with that perplexity; this is the next step up, namely, how can we systematically approach the Bible.

We ourselves, the authors of this book, have agonized over this question for many years. It has bothered us that we ourselves have been guilty of applying certain passages vigorously while glibly ignoring others. We believe that we have come upon a consistent approach, an algorithm if you will, for applying statements from the Bible to our lives today as modern followers of Jesus the Messiah. In a later chapter we will set out that algorithm again and begin to elucidate it, but before we do, one more word about algorithms. An algorithm is a method which one can use over and over again to get what is needed. It's not subjective; it is an objective standard, like a ruler or a measuring cup. A mathematical formula can be an algorithm. If a builder or an engineer has devised a formula for the design of a certain part of the project, a formula which can be used repeatedly to get just the right fit, then that's an algorithm. An algorithm, though never perfect (nothing in this world is), approaches exactness and minimizes the emotional component. If a word processing program allowed its user to find every word in a document which began with the letters "Jes", it would use an algorithm to do it. We believe we can offer and defend an algorithm for selecting just those teachings, principles and practices in the Bible which are meant for all disciples of Jesus for all times, all places and for all cultures.

2 Some Current Proposed Solutions

The sign says "BRIDGE OUT AHEAD". Ignoring that sign could result in some serious problems. There are warning signs in our journey of faith, also. When we see the sign on the side of the trail that says "INCONSISTENCY", we should not make the mistake of ignoring that sign. Inconsistency is not a little problem. As Jesus said, God's word is truth (John 17.17). If God's word is truth, it is not inconsistent. When we find ourselves applying passages of scripture inconsistently to our lives, it serves as a warning that something is wrong. As Todd Deaver told his religious constituency, it will not do to admit that applying the Bible is a thorny issue. It will not do, he said, because their way of doing so was, not just difficult, but inconsistent.[1] He had seen the warning sign on the side of the road. Inconsistency meant they were doing something wrong. "Brethren," he added, "we are in plain self-contradiction. . . . . There is no rational way we can simply dismiss

---

1 Deaver, *op. cit.*, p. 105.

this as a minor problem and carry on with business as usual."[2] His circumstances, by his own admission, were extreme, but he is not alone in inconsistency. As we saw in the previous chapter, most followers of Christ lack a consistent system of applying teachings from the Bible to their lives. It is our aim in this chapter to critique some current attempts at solving the problem. In the paragraphs that follow we want to set out some of these approaches, but we want to make it clear that any particular Bible reader might not necessarily fall into one of these categories. We might have overlooked some approach. Or, one might find himself in one or more of these categories that have been blended together.

Proposed Solution #1 – The General Wisdom Approach

First of all, there are those, of course, who see the Bible as classic literature. They read the Bible very much like one would read Homer's *Iliad* or *Odyssey*. That is, they view it as a grand story that incorporates certain classic values; the question of whether the story is true or not is not even relevant to them. These interpreters would say that there are certain great human values that can be found in the classics of human civilization and that these values can be used in our lives today to inform our decisions and behaviors. This approach, in fact, broaches a very important question, namely, why should one think that the Bible applied to him when it wasn't written to him in the first place? One wouldn't do that with the *Iliad*.

Now, the question we are addressing in this book would not be relevant to those people who read the Bible with The General Wisdom Approach. But for many of us who think (as we do) that the Bible does indeed record the acts of God in history and does indeed reveal God's truths as given by and to certain people at certain times, the question of how to apply the Bible to our lives becomes a vital issue. The General Wisdom Approach to the Bible is not a live option for us. People who read the Bible as classical literature would feel perfectly free to dispense with certain values they find in the Bible when they perceive them to be outdated and irrelevant. This type of reader might even feel that the modern perspective is so superior that he is not constrained to accept

---

2 *Ibid.*, p.108.

any of the values he finds in the Bible, nor of any other classic literature. In effect, this approach is highly subjective. Yet, there is a sting to
this approach, because that is in fact what many Christians do with the
Bible, after all. We too sometimes have felt perfectly free to ignore certain verses in the Bible, even when they can be found adjacent to verses
which we believe are the word of God. The approach of devoted Christians to the Bible has often been very subjective. So even though very,
very few Christians would admittedly approach the Bible according to
the classical literature view, this approach does have some illustrative
value with regard to the question of this book.

Let's now look at some other approaches.

Proposed Solution #2 – Hermeneutics Unnecessary

Another approach would be simply to dismiss the questions of
hermeneutics altogether. This approach sees the question of how to apply the Bible to our lives as unnecessary, if not problematic. There is the
natural human desire towards simplicity: why cannot one simply read
his Bible, believe it and then just do what it says? But the whole reason
for this book is that that has been tried for many years, and it has turned
out to be much more difficult than anticipated, as we saw in the previous
chapter.

One is reminded at this point of Plato's' dialogue "Euthyphro",
in which the young Euthyphro is accosted by the older Socrates, as the
former is coming out of the courts. Euythphro has just brought suit
against his father for murder and seems to be quite confident about his
decision to do so. Socrates, always coming from a philosophical disposition, asks the confident Euthyphro what hermeneutic he used to decide
what is good and what is evil. As Plato' readers know, Euthyphro reflected a complete lack of any awareness of how he arrived at his conclusions about good behavior and bad behavior. He had no hermeneutic
at all; he had no answer to Socrates as to how he arrived at the decision
to prosecute his father.

We are suggesting that many Bible readers today are in Euthyphro's position. They would argue, vociferously in fact, that certain
behaviors are divinely required and divinely condemned. When asked
how they arrive at those conclusions, they would probably respond that

the Bible makes such conclusions perfectly clear. These people would go on to say that the philosophical question of hermeneutics is distractive, serving only to get us off the track of what we should be doing and that we should be wary of this question just as we are wary of the devil's other temptations. These fine God fearing people (and we use these adjectives sincerely) want to believe what they should believe and do what they should do, and they worry that raising such philosophical questions might lure them away from their dedication to God. There is a name for this position; it is called presuppositionalism, which in this case says that the Christian worldview is a package deal, that one presupposes its truth, and then bases one's life upon it. They might insist that worldviews cannot be proven to be true or false. They might also contend that such philosophical questions are simply beyond our ability to answer. So the question of how we arrive at what is true or false, or obligatory or not, is simply beyond our ken.

However, as we can see from the discussion in Chapter 1, there are some who see problems in how we have used the Bible and have legitimate questions concerning such. We see those problems too, and we wish to address them. So, in the spirit of that concern, we suggest that there are some problems with presupposing the biblical worldview.

First of all, worldviews are like driving a stake into the ground and then tethering ourselves to that stake. From that vantage point we are able to look out at the rest of the world and to assess the world from that perspective. The problem, of course, is that the stake can be driven into any number of spots, each of which will become a different perspective on the rest of the world. So, that raises the question as to which, or whose, perspective is the correct one. Some would say that worldviews are incommensurable, that is, that one can never ask whether one worldview is superior to another. But the problem with this approach is that it is closed minded and shuts down all discussion of the matter. The very definition of closed minded is that one has accepted a point of view and refuses to critique it or revise it. When two people view reality from two different worldview perspectives (which happens often), there is simply no way for the two different people to have a meaningful discussion. Muslims have one worldview, secularists have another. Mormons have their way, and evangelicals have their own point of view. Many other worldviews could be listed here. If we don't raise the question of what method we are using to get from the Bible to our beliefs and practices today, then we are forever closed off, each group in our own little world.

Perhaps an illustration would be helpful, in fact, a famous illustration. Around 150 AD Claudius Ptolemy devised a very complicated system for predicting the movements of celestial entities, such as planets, moons and stars, based on the assumption (his stake in the ground) that the earth was the center of what we now call the solar system. Later, in the 16th century the Copernicus brothers, much to the dismay of European scholars, advanced a cosmological theory based on the assumption (their stake in the ground) that the sun was the center. Now, it is important to know that both systems worked well with regard to predicting the movements of the celestial bodies, though the Copernican system was far, far simpler. For centuries the two theories were incommensurable, that is, there was no objective way to determine which of the two, if either, was true. Was the earth the center of all the celestial bodies in its locality, or was the sun? In the modern age of advanced science and space travel, the Copernican view has been demonstrated to be true. Similarly, we might ask whether the various religious worldviews, like Hinduism and Judeo-Christianity, are simply incommensurable, with no way to determine which of the two is most likely true. And this brings us back to our hermeneutical question: is each Bible reader simply consigned by historical accident to a particular traditional way of extracting principles from the texts, or is there a way to extract those principles which is superior to the other ways?

It is interesting to note that presuppositionalism was not the practice of the early church. When one reads the sermons in the New Testament, one finds Paul and the other writers making a case for the truth of the gospel and how that truth makes a difference in one's life. When one reads Tertullian, Justin Martyr, or Aristides, one is struck by the vigor that these early Christians evinced in their efforts to show that the new worldview found in Jesus is correct and superior to other worldviews. Apparently, they were not postmodernists; they did not believe that worldviews are incommensurable. Furthermore, neither did they believe that just any interpretation of the basic teachings of Christianity was as good as any other. So, among Bible reading Christians today, there are many competing systems of beliefs and practices. Just as with the example of worldviews, the question of how we arrive at our conclusions must be raised. If every different hermeneutic for reading and applying the texts of the Bible is as good as any other, then all discussion as to the truth of the Bible is over.

Proposed Solution #3 – Tradition

Now, some people just choose to follow their particular traditions. After all, they have known so many good people inside their traditions. However, the problem of hermeneutics is still not solved. After all, these good people disagree, greatly. It is indeed understandable how people might come to revere a certain church leader so highly that they never question his or her judgment. We respect tradition, there is some value to it; but it does not answer our question, namely, what in fact is the best algorithm for applying biblical teachings?

Proposed Solution #4 – The Great Thinkers Approach

Similarly, there are those who retort that all of the great teaching and principles have already been established, in fact, established by greater minds than our minds. To these people our question comes across as the height of arrogance. Origen, Augustine, Aquinas and Calvin have spoken on these matters, and we modern folk are in no position to gainsay their renderings. Surely, these names are familiar to us today because of the great contributions their bearers made to the history of Christianity. But would it be too much to ask what hermeneutical algorithm they used to draw their conclusions? This algorithm is what we are looking for.

Proposed Solution #5 – Inconsistent Failures

There are those who have been a part of a religious group which has indeed tried to come up with a hermeneutical algorithm. We ourselves are a part of such a group. So is Todd Deaver, who was discussed above. The people in such groups are trying to use a system when they apply passages from the Bible to their practices as a group, as well as to their practices as individual Christians. They're trying to be consistent. For example, in our heritage there developed some heart rending schisms over certain practices. A hermeneutic was devised, post hoc we believe (actually, it was borrowed from the early Protestant Reformation), that went something like this. Nothing is permissible unless it could be shown in the Bible to be straightforwardly commanded, or shown by a biblical example to be allowable or to be necessary as a result of inference. As a newcomer to this idea might guess, this hermeneutic proved over time to be impossible. If our fellowship had indeed applied it in a thoroughgoing consistent manner, we would have had no church buildings, no songbooks, no cars, no TV or internet programs, and everyone would have given everything they had to the poor. This is the point of Deaver's book, *Facing Our Failures*. Not only was the hermeneutic under his consideration applied inconsistently (as it had to be), but the idea of a "necessary inference" turned out to be a catchall for any practice one might want to preserve. We admire people who have striven to devise a hermeneutic, but we just haven't found one that consistently works--until now.

Proposed Solution #6 – Common Sense

Another sector of believers would be those who have simply settled on their beliefs and practices, and since these things make sense to them they do not wish to be disturbed about them. They often have some kind of hermeneutic, but it goes undefended. In fact, if there are things which do not fit comfortably into their traditions, or if inconsistencies in the application of their hermeneutic are pointed out, they simply brush them aside. One can usually find this group by their catchphrases. For example, when some of the things we mentioned in Chapter 1, such as the Sabbath, tithing, foot washing, charismatic gifts and women wearing head coverings, are brought up, one is met with responses like, "Don't be ridiculous", "You have to use some common sense", "As we all know, . . .", or "Be reasonable". These, of course, are not answers. Neither do they represent an algorithm for applying passages to our lives.

This approach might seem to be the same as Proposal #3 – Tradition, but this group would not appeal to tradition; it appeals instead to common sense. But what exactly is common sense, and how does it work in solving our problem? In fact, common sense is a very nebulous term and is usually referred to when in fact there is no algorithm for finding an answer.

Proposed Solution #7 – Mysticism

A very widespread approach to the problem of how to apply the Bible to our lives is the mystical one. This is especially true with those who take a very strong stand on the active work of the Holy Spirit in the heart of the believer. It also fits very well in our postmodern, relativistic time in which we live. Since this is an inner approach, there is no objective algorithm to be found in it. Within this approach there are those who would say, "The Bible is a living document; it can mean something quite different to each different individual reader."

The question we are raising in this book, then, would not be a question for these people, and our solution would be irrelevant. The problem, of course, with this view is that it is totally subjective. At the end of the day, a reader could maintain that he got anything out of his encounter with the Bible, no matter how outlandishly bizarre it might be, and there would be no way even to suggest that he might be mistaken. There are simply no controls on interpretation and application on this approach, neither history, lexicography nor logic.

Proposed Solution #8 – Holy Spirit Guided

This next one is similar to Solution #7. There are those, as we saw in Chapter 1, who are aware of widespread inconsistency in our use of the scriptures, are bothered by it (unlike the mystics) and have attempted to find solutions. However, they often conjoin to their methodology the assurance that the Holy Spirit is guiding them in efforts to get from the Bible to their daily lives.

Scot McKnight, for example, leans heavily on the concept of discernment, which he admits is a "grey and fuzzy area". "The pattern of discernment is simply this: as we read the Bible and locate each item in its place in the Story, as we listen to God speak to us in our world through God's ancient Word, we discern – *through God's Spirit and in the context of our community of faith – a pattern of how to live **in our*** *world".*[3] This is a very common view. We suspect, in fact, that the relativism of the present postmodern period has contributed to this reliance on the Holy Spirit.

However, while we appreciate much of what McKnight has to say, we find his offerings short of the mark. Different communities of faith have notoriously differed on the application of the biblical texts, giving rise, in fact, to the very question of this book; the problem of how to apply the teachings to our world is again just the problem. But exactly what are the methods and principles involved in discernment? Though McKnight seems to mean that believers can extract principles from the story of the Bible, and that is not so fuzzy, we are still left at the end with no idea of just exactly how we know which principles apply, nor which statements of doctrine are salvation issues nor which practices are obligatory. Neither does McKnight's reliance on the Holy Spirit help. Reliance on the Spirit is often claimed, but the results have been wildly varied. Many people claim that their many and varied applications of the scriptures were given to them by the Spirit. Sometimes people claim to be led by the Spirit to believe or do things that most Christians are quite convinced are contrary to very plain commandments in the Scriptures. Others sometimes draw Spirit-led conclusions which conflict with those drawn by others. And sometimes people claim to have received revelation through the Holy Spirit, instructing others in their fellowship to make serious changes in their lives. Actually, though, this amounts to subjectivism.[4] Without an objective methodology, how would these putative Spirit-led revelations be properly assessed?[5] In brief, we didn't find in McKnight's book an answer to our question.

---

3 - *Ibid.*, p. 129. Italics and bold print are his.

4 An interesting discussion of the problems inherent in this proposed solution can be found in *Led by the Spirit, Toward a Practical Theology of Pentacostal Discernment and Decision Making*, by Stephen E. Parker, a professor of counseling and a Pentacostal Christian. Sheffield: Sheffield Academic Press, 1996.

5 See Gary T. Cage, *The Holy Spirit, A Sourcebook with Commentary*, Reno, NV: Charlotte House Publishers, 1995, or the condensed version, *Clothed with Power, A Brief Study of the Indwelling of the Holy Spirit*, Reno, NV: Charlotte House Publishers, 1996.

Proposal #9 – Principle Based

Grant R. Osborne's very fine book, *The Hermeneutical Spiral*, is a comprehensive study of the whole matter of interpreting scripture. Most of the book is about matters such as philosophies of interpretation, the role of history and culture, principles of literary criticism and mundane things like grammar, lexicography and syntax. But at one point he takes up the issue of how to apply the scriptures to our lives, which he says is the ultimate goal of hermeneutics, after all. Osborne takes a very modest stance on the role of the Holy Spirit, suggesting that the Spirit opens the mind and the will of the reader, without telling him how to apply the meaning of the text to his life. Then he suggests four principles for applying the text. First, one needs to understand the text in its original historical and cultural context. Second, the interpreter should find the operative principles the original writer was using. Third, Osborne suggests meditation. And lastly, the reader should find parallels between his circumstances and the circumstances of the original audience.[6] Osborne's is a principle-based approach and is in fact the way most people use the Bible. But still we are left with a lack of clarity. How do we derive those principles? Do all principles found in the Bible apply to us today? And are the only things that apply to us today principles; what about certain overt behaviors, or even rituals?

A similar principle-based approach is Richard B. Hays' beautiful work, *The Moral Vision of the New Testament*. Admittedly, he does not set out to answer our question but rather to apply biblical principles to current issues, but he does stop along the way to ask how we believers are to use the texts. To find those all-important biblical principles Hays says we need to respect the total biblical context, listen to and weigh tradition, use reason with caution, consider the broad experience of all Christ followers, and finally, to employ imagination. This last item is extremely germane to our concerns. Hays says, "Such imaginative integration would not be necessary if it were possible to separate out 'timeless truth' in the New Testament from 'culturally conditioned' elements." Though Hays says that the effort to distinguish those time-

---

6 Grant R. Osborne, *The Hermeneutical Spiral, A Comprehensive Introduction to Biblical Interpretation,* Downers Grove, IL: InterVarsity Press, 1991, pp.344-347

less truths is "wrongheaded and impossible"[7], that is just exactly what we think we can and must do.

Conclusion

Many have been concerned with the issue of how to go from the Bible to our individual lives, as well as to the corporate life of the church. We truly respect the efforts of those who have wrestled with this problem, but after surveying the offerings, we believe that we have come up empty handed. Though some, for various reasons, have employed some rather bizarre approaches to the subject, it appears to be true that most people find some way to apply principles from the Bible. That also is admirable, but we want to do better than that. We seek an actual algorithm by which we can discern just what parts of the Bible are applicable to all Christ followers from century to century, in every part of the world and in every different culture. Though we realize that applying principles in itself is difficult and that that problem will probably never be avoided, it would seem that the very first step is to be able to isolate those principles, commands and rituals which are meant to be universal in the first place. The average Bible reader needs a method for determining which teachings are incumbent upon him, and to that we now turn.

We need to prepare you. The next few chapters are a bit strenuous. We're going to present our algorithm, explain in detail how we arrived at it, expand upon it, test it and defend it against some objections before we summarize it and show what it means to us today. In the next chapter we're going to present The Kingdom Algorithm. We intend to show how the kingdom of God is the basis of the gospel and why the kingdom should be our paradigm for applying the gospel to our lives.

---

7 Richard B. Hayes, *The Moral Vision of the New Testament, Community, Cross, New Creation, A Contemporary Introduction to New Testament Ethics,* San Francisco: HarperCollins Publishers, 1996, pp. 290-312.

3 The Kingdom As Basic

Simply stated, the algorithm is this: whatever one finds in the Bible as inextricably essential to the spiritual kingdom of Christ is essential for all Christians for all time; otherwise not. This is our algorithm. This principle is what we believe should be used to get from the Bible to our lives today as disciples of Christ. Given the problem set out in Chapter One and the failures to solve it, as set out in the above chapters, we considered the possibility of a new approach. We believe this algorithm of how to apply the Bible to our lives emerges from the texts having to do with the Kingdom of God.

The Bible is a narrative. From beginning to end there is a story being told, a story about God's plan, His great acts in history and His interaction with human beings, culminating in the mission of Jesus the Christ. That story is so bold and so central in the Bible that it must reveal God's aims for us. It appears that Jesus' mission was to set up an eternal and spiritual kingdom and to call people from all times and places into that kingdom. So, in the next few chapters we want to set out what we have found in the scriptures to be the essential characteristics of the kingdom of Christ. We shall proceed by going through the scriptures, topically, to set out those essential characteristics. In this chapter and the next two, we will mention every text in the New Testament which explicitly mentions the kingdom. After that, we will provide a concise description of the modern day universal citizen of the kingdom. We will also make a list of obvious things that are not essential to citizenship in Jesus' kingdom today, since the long history of the church has seen quite an accrual of doctrines and practices, most of which have been issues of contention. Then, before concluding with a statement as to what this all means, we will attempt to test the algorithm and deal with objections that might be raised to our algorithm. This chapter will be confined to the four gospels and what they say about Jesus' mission to set up an eternal, spiritual kingdom for God.

The Kingdom of God in the Old Testament

We wish we could give the space to this topic which it deserves, but suffice it to say here that God was recognized as King at least as early as His victory over the Egyptians at the Red Sea (Exodus 15.18). When the people later asked Samuel for a human king, God saw them as rejecting Him as their spiritual King (1 Samuel 8.7). After the disaster that was King Saul, God placed David on the throne and established his lineage forever (2 Samuel 7.11b-16):

Moreover, the Lord declares to you that the Lord will make you a house. When your days are fulfilled and you lie down with your fathers, I will raise up your offspring after you, who shall come from your body, and I will establish his kingdom. He shall build a house for my name, and I will establish the throne of his kingdom forever. I will be to him a father, and he shall be to me a son. When he commits iniquity, I will discipline him with the rod of men, with the stripes of the sons of men, but my steadfast love will not depart from him, as I took it from Saul, whom I put away from before you. And your house and your kingdom shall be made sure forever before me. Your throne shall be established forever.

As all students of the Bible know, though David did fairly well, most of his successors did not, until God removed the kings through the destruction of Jerusalem by the Babylonians in 586 BC. But Jeremiah had promised the Jews a resurrection of the Davidic line (Jeremiah 23.5-6). Therefore, the lengthy series of controllers and oppressors did nothing but create a deep longing for the Messiah to come, one who would once again rule in righteousness over Israel. This is why the debate over Jesus often centered on whether he was the king of the Jews (Matthew 2.2, 27.6-16, 27-44, Mark 15.2-32, Luke 23.1-5, 33-43). The angel told Mary that her son would sit on the throne of David (Luke 1.32). And at Jesus' final entrance into the city of Jerusalem the people welcomed Jesus as king, calling him "the son of David" (Matthew 21.1-9, Mark 11.1-10, Luke 19.28-38). This is a brief description of the kingdom of God in the Old Testament, but it serves to give the background of Jesus' ministry.

The Kingdom as the Aim of Jesus' Mission

In the New Testament, the kingdom of God is the reason for which Jesus came.[1] Even the casual reader of the New Testament is struck by how the mission of Christ revolves around the kingdom of God.[2] The kingdom is central to the gospel message. This kingdom is also presented as the culmination of everything God had begun with Abraham, Moses, and the people of Israel. In fact, as Matthew states, it was prepared by God at the "foundation of the world" (25.34). So, Jesus' spiritual kingdom can be said to be God's eternal plan for the ages.

That is why John the Baptizer introduced Jesus by announcing the coming of the kingdom (Matthew 3.1-2). However, John saw himself as only the harbinger of the one who would indeed usher in the

---

1 As many Bible commentators have noted, the kingdom of God is the same as the kingdom of heaven. One can see this when one turns to the Gospel of Matthew and sees the phrase "the kingdom of heaven" used over and over, but the parallels in the Gospel of Mark consistently use the phrase "the kingdom of God". The terms are interchangeable.

2 In a standard edition of the synoptic gospels, Matthew, Mark and Luke organized in parallel columns (for example Burton H. Throckmorton, Jr., ed., *Gospel Parallels, A synopsis of the First Three Gospels,* Nashville. Thomas Nelson Publishers, 4th ed., revised, 1979), there are usually about 270 divisions of the texts into pericopes, parables and teaching sections. Fully 80 or more of these are explicitly about Jesus' mission to set up the kingdom, and many more have undertones of the kingdom message because of their proximity to the 80.

kingdom. The whole first chapter in the Gospel of John is given over to the transfer of the mission, along with a few disciples, from the Baptizer to the coming Messiah. Now, it is true that the concept of the kingdom of God does not explicitly play a preeminent role in Fourth Gospel terminology, like it does in the synoptic gospels, however we do find a few explicit statements about it, and they are very significant. In the very opening chapter of the Gospel of John, we find Jesus accumulating disciples. One of these disciples is Nathaniel, and upon becoming convinced of the special role that Jesus had, Nathaniel exclaimed, "Rabbi, you are the Son of God! You are the King of Israel!" (John 1.49).

Then, almost immediately, Jesus arrives on the public scene and begins his ministry, but, and this is very important, the theme of the mission does not change; the kingdom remains central. Matthew makes a point of it, "From that time Jesus began to preach, saying, 'Repent, for the kingdom of heaven is at hand'" (4.23-25). This shows that the early public ministry of Jesus was all about this kingdom of heaven, which was eminent and which had already been the subject of John's preaching.[3]

Shortly thereafter, after Jesus had spent the whole night healing people, "he departed and went into a desolate place. And the people sought him and came to him, and would have kept him from leaving them, but he said to them, "I must preach the good news of the kingdom of God to the other towns as well; for I was sent for this purpose" (Luke 4.42-43). Here is an explicit statement as to the aims of Jesus. The message of the kingdom had priority over everything else, Jesus' healing ministry as well as Jesus' need for rest.

Jesus continued to fulfill his mission and even made it the mission of his disciples (Matthew 9.35-10.16; cf. Luke 9.1-6):

And Jesus went throughout all the cities and villages, teaching in their synagogues and proclaiming the gospel of the kingdom and healing every disease and

---

3 As has often been noted, the Gospel of Matthew can be divided into two broad sections, one beginning in Mathew 4.17 and the second starting in 16.21. Each of these sections starts with the phrase "From that time". In the second section of Matthew it says that the latter part of Jesus' ministry had to do with preparing his immediate disciples for his demise, but the first part of Jesus' ministry had to do with the imminent arrival of the kingdom of heaven.

every affliction. When he saw the crowds, he had compassion for them, because they were harassed and helpless, like sheep without a shepherd. Then he said to his disciples, "The harvest is plentiful, but the laborers are few; therefore pray earnestly to the Lord of the harvest to send out laborers into his harvest." And he called to him his twelve disciples and gave them authority over unclean spirits, to cast them out, and to heal every disease and every affliction. The names of the twelve apostles are these: first, Simon, who is called Peter, and Andrew his brother; James the son of Zebedee, and John his brother; Philip and Bartholomew; Thomas and Matthew the tax collector; James the son of Alphaeus, and Thaddaeus; Simon the Zealot, and Judas Iscariot, who betrayed him. These twelve Jesus sent out, instructing them, "Go nowhere among the Gentiles and enter no town of the Samaritans, but go rather to the lost sheep of the house of Israel. And proclaim as you go, saying, 'The kingdom of heaven is at hand.' Heal the sick, raise the dead, cleanse lepers, cast out demons. You received without paying; give without pay. Acquire no gold or silver or copper for your belts, no bag for your journey, or two tunics or sandals or a staff, for the laborer deserves his food. And whatever town or village you enter, find out who is worthy in it and stay there until you depart.

We suggest that one of the clearest ways to see what was central to Jesus is to see what he transferred to his immediate disciples.

But let's return to the Gospel of John. According to the Fourth Gospel, at the end of Jesus' ministry, Pilate interviewed Jesus, and the author of the Fourth Gospel tells it this way (18.33-38):

So Pilate entered his headquarters again and called Jesus and said to him, "Are you the King of the Jews?" Jesus answered, "Do you say this of your own accord, or did others say it to you about me?" Pilate answered, "Am I a Jew? Your own nation and the chief priests have delivered you over to me. What have you done?" Jesus answered, "My kingdom is not of this world. If my kingdom were of this world, my servants would have been fighting, that I might not be delivered over to the Jews. But my kingdom is not from the world." Then Pilate said to him, "So you are a king?" Jesus answered, "You say that I am a king. For this purpose I was born and for this purpose I have come into the world—to bear witness to the truth. Everyone who is of the truth listens to my voice." Pilate said to him, "What is truth?" After he had said this, he went back outside to the Jews and told them, "I find no guilt in him."

This is an extraordinarily important passage for the question of this book. Jesus is saying that the reason that he came into this world was to set up a kingdom which is not of this world. It is a spiritual kingdom. It is not involved in militarism, politics or human power. And this also brings us to the point about truth. Jesus connected his kingdom to truth. It has often been noticed by readers of this gospel that the concept of truth plays a big role in its picture of Jesus. Let's look at a few examples of this. In John 4, in a discussion with a Samaritan woman, Jesus defined real worship, that is genuine worship, and it had nothing to do with time or place. Jesus said in vs. 23, "But the hour is coming, and now is, when the true worshipers will worship the Father in spirit and truth, for such the Father seeks to worship him. God is spirit and those who worship him must worship in spirit and truth." Jesus connected true worship there with his kingdom, which was about to come into the world. The citizens of this new spiritual kingdom would be worshiping God without regard to time or place, but instead worshiping God with their lives. A similar passage is John 8.31-32, where Jesus said, "If you abide in my word, you are truly my disciples, and you will know the truth, and the truth will set you free." In the context, Jesus was making a point that it was not merely being a Jew that counted with God but living out godly principles in one's life. And a third exemplary passage is John 14.6 where Jesus said, "I am the way, and the truth, and the life. No one comes to the Father except through me." It appears that for the author of the Fourth Gospel, Jesus came to give people a transcendent truth, the big picture, of what God is all about. This truth can be found in Jesus' eternal, spiritual kingdom, and it is the main reason for which Jesus came in to this world.

Finally, we note, Jesus was empowered by the Holy Spirit to work miracles, the purpose of which was to demonstrate that he was there truly to usher in the kingdom of God. As he said on one occasion (Luke 11.17-23, cf. Matt 12.25-37, Mark 3.23-30):

> Every kingdom divided against itself is laid waste, and no city or house divided against itself will stand. And if Satan casts out Satan, he is divided against himself. How then will his kingdom stand? And if I cast out demons by Beelzebul, by whom do your sons cast them out? Therefore they will be your judges. But if it is by the Spirit of God that I cast out demons, then the kingdom of God has come upon you. Or how can someone enter a strong man's house and plunder his goods, unless he first binds the strong man? Then indeed he may plunder his house. Whoever is not with me is against me, and whoever does not gather with me scatters. Therefore I tell you, every sin and blasphemy will be forgiven people, but the blasphemy against the Spirit will not be forgiven. And whoever speaks a word against the Son of Man will be forgiven, but whoever speaks against the Holy Spirit will not be forgiven, either in this age or in the age to come. Either make the tree good and its fruit good, or make the tree bad and its fruit bad, for the tree is known by its fruit. You brood of vipers! How can you speak good, when you are evil? For out of the abundance of the heart the mouth speaks. The good person out of his good treasure brings forth good, and the evil person out of his evil treasure brings forth evil. I tell you, on the day of judgment people will give account for every careless word they speak, for by your words you will be justified, and by your words you will be condemned.

So we can confidently say, at this point, that Jesus' central aim in coming into this world was to usher in and establish the final state of God's kingdom.

The Spiritual Nature of the Kingdom

As the previous passage says, Jesus was at war, not with human kingdoms, but with the kingdom of Satan, and that is because Jesus' kingdom itself is spiritual, not earthly. One of the biggest tensions in the ministry of Jesus was about the Jewish expectation of a physical kingdom, like that of David and Solomon's, as opposed to the spiritual kingdom which Jesus came to establish. But Jesus' kingdom does contrast with human kingdoms, like the empire of Rome, or even the kingdom of David; it has no central headquarters on earth, no human king sitting on a throne, and no physical military force to enforce its laws.

A very revealing episode, in this regard, is the one in which the imprisoned John the Baptizer sent two of his disciples to Jesus to inquire about his mission (Matthew 11.2-19; cf. Luke 7.18-35):

As they went away, Jesus began to speak to the crowds concerning John: "What did you go out into the wilderness to see? A reed shaken by the wind? What then did you go out to see? A man dressed in soft clothing? Behold, those who wear soft clothing are in kings' houses. What then did you go out to see? A prophet? Yes, I tell you, and more than a prophet. This is he of whom it is written,

Behold, I send my messenger before your face, who will prepare your way before you.

Truly, I say to you, among those born of women there has arisen no one greater than John the Baptist. Yet the one who is least in the kingdom of heaven is greater than he. From the days of John the Baptist until now the kingdom of heaven has suffered violence, and the violent take it by force. For all the Prophets and the Law prophesied until John, and if you are willing to accept it, he is Elijah who is to come. He who has ears to hear, let him hear."

It appears that even John himself struggled with the nature of the kingdom. Even though John had carried out his mission well, he did not realize that the kingdom was spiritual. Like the many who saw it in militaristic terms, perhaps even John expected Jesus to be an earthly ruler. This is why Jesus spoke of the "secrets of the kingdom of heaven" (Matthew 13.10, Mark 4.11, Luke 8.9). Until one could accept the spiritual nature of the kingdom, Jesus' message would remain a mystery. Jesus spoke a parable about this (Mark 2.26-29):

> The kingdom of God is as if a man should scatter seed on the ground. He sleeps and rises night and day, and the seed sprouts and grows; he knows not how. The earth produces by itself, first the blade, then the ear, then the full grain in the ear. But when the grain is ripe, at once he puts in the sickle, because the harvest has come.

Just as God manages agriculture from behind the scenes, He also grows the kingdom in an unseen way.

Matthew 13, the third major discourse of his gospel, contains most of the parables of the kingdom, the most important of which would be the Parable of the Sower. These parables were used by Jesus to prepare his most immediate disciples for the task before them, namely, presenting the gospel of the kingdom to the next generation. Here is the Parable of the Sower 13.1-9, cf. Mark 4.1-9 and Luke 4.4-8):

> A sower went out to sow. And as he s o w e d , some seeds fell along the path, and the birds came and devoured them. Other seeds fell on rocky ground, where they did not have much soil, and immediately they sprang up, since they had no depth of soil, but when the sun rose they were scorched. And since they had no root, they withered away. Other seeds fell among thorns, and the thorns grew up and choked them. Other seeds fell on good soil and produced grain, some a hundredfold, some sixty, some thirty. He who has ears, let him hear."

And then the interpretation (Matthew 13.18-23; cf. Mark 4.13-20, Luke 8.11-15):

> Hear then the parable of the sower: When anyone hears the word of the kingdom and does not understand it, the evil one comes and snatches away what has been sown in his heart. This is what was sown along the path. As for what was sown on rocky ground, this is the one who hears the word and immediately receives it

with joy, yet he has no root in himself, but endures for
a while, and when tribulation or persecution arises on
account of the word, immediately he falls away. As for
what was sown among thorns, this is the one who hears
the word, but the cares of the world and the deceitfulness
of riches choke the word, and it proves unfruitful. As for
what was sown on good soil, this is the one who hears
the word and understands it. He indeed bears fruit and
yields, in one case a hundredfold, in another sixty, and
in another thirty."

The successful hearer of the word of the kingdom would be one who
could understand the spiritual nature of the kingdom and would continue to pursue it, thereby bringing forth much fruit.

But one of the boldest moments for this tension between the
physical conception of the kingdom and the spiritual conception was the
episode of the Feeding of the Five Thousand (Matthew 14.13-21, Mark
6.30-44, Luke 9.10-17, John 6.1-71). For years it has been a scholarly
consensus that this episode was actually about a conflict over the nature
of the kingdom. Jesus had sent his disciples to preach, but while they
were out there King Herod executed John the Baptizer, so adored by the
people. This created a political excitement which resulted in the disciples gathering up about 5,000 men (no women and children) ready for
battle.[4] Jesus tried to get away from the crowd, "for many were coming
and going, and they had no leisure even to eat" (Mark 6.31); but the
throng followed him and his immediate disciples. Jesus quelled the up-
roar by feeding the army miraculously (and then escaping), but before
he departed, "he spoke to them about the kingdom of God" (Luke 9.11).
The people were extremely impressed with the feeding miracle. "When
the people saw the sign that he had done, they said, 'This is indeed the
Prophet who is to come into the world!' Perceiving then that they were
about to come and take him by force to make him king, Jesus withdrew
again to the mountain by himself" (John 6.14-15). Some of Jesus' hearers compared Jesus to Moses in the wilderness with the Israelites, but:

Jesus then said to them, "Truly, truly, I say to you,
it was not Moses who gave you the bread from heaven,

---

4 Hugh Montefiore, "Revolt in the Desert?", *New Testament Studies*, VIII (January,
1965), pp.135-141.

but my Father gives you the true bread from heaven. For the bread of God is he who comes down from heaven and gives life to the world." They said to him, "Sir, give us this bread always" (John 6.32-34).

Jesus, of course, meant his message: "It is written in the Prophets, 'And they will all be taught by God.' Everyone who has heard and learned from the Father comes to me" (John 6.45). Then concluding, he said, "It is the Spirit who gives life; the flesh is no help at all. The words that I have spoken to you are spirit and life" (John 6.63). Unfortunately, the people's paradigm was fleshly, so they were not ready to accept Jesus' meaning. We are then told that the many turned away from Jesus after this point (John 6.66). Also reflected in this account, as in so many parts of the gospels, is the inability of Jesus' own immediate disciples to get their minds around the spiritual nature of the kingdom. The problem was that Jesus' kingdom was spiritual, and they were fleshly.

In fact, Jesus died because of this flesh/spirit tension. Jesus' enemies used the kingdom issue to get Jesus arrested, since Governor Pilate's hand would be forced by a claim to kingship (Mt 25.11; cf. Mark 15.2, Luke 23.3):

> Now Jesus stood before the governor, and the governor asked him, "Are you the King of the Jews?"
> Jesus said, "You have said so."

Overall, Jesus was quite taciturn, so the governor offered to release a prisoner he had captured, called Barabbas. But even the choice of the freedom fighter Barabbas reflected the people's militaristic view of the coming kingdom.[5] The governor delivered Jesus to the soldiers, who mocked him and led him out to be crucified. The titulum attached to the top of the cross read, "This is Jesus, the King of the Jews" (Matthew 27.37). The Jewish leaders also mocked him (Matthew 27.42-43),"He is the King of Israel; let him come down now from the cross, and we will believe in him. . . . . For he said, "I am the Son of God." All of this shows in a very graphic way how different Jesus' concept of the

---

5 Unlike the usual representation of him, Barabbas was not a common thug; he was a freedom fighter. He was a first century Jewish "Robin Hood". In fact, Barabbas was not his name; it was an appellation, meaning "son of the father". Barabbas was probably a son, or a close follower, of a prominent rebel leader. He himself was deeply involved in insurrection (Luke 23:19), so of course the Jews preferred the release of Barabbas over Jesus' release.

kingdom was from that of his contemporaries. The Jews of Jesus' day sought an earthly kingdom where the king would sit on a physical throne and rule his empire with military force from a central geographical location. Little did Pilate and the Jews of that day realize that they were indeed crucifying the real king of God's kingdom, a king who would rule from heaven over an eternal and spiritual domain.

Finally, there are the words from Jesus on the cross (Luke 23.39-43):

> One of the criminals who were hanged railed at him, saying, "Are you not the Christ? Save yourself and us!" But the other rebuked him, saying, "Do you not fear God, since you are under the same sentence of condemnation? And we indeed justly, for we are receiving the due reward of our deeds; but this man has done nothing wrong." And he said, "Jesus, remember me when you come into your kingdom." And he said to him, "Truly, I say to you, today you will be with me in Paradise."

The words of the second criminal reflect a significant paradigm shift in the perspective of the kingdom. And Jesus' reply certainly indicates his understanding of the kingdom as spiritual, with him as the king ruling from heaven.

Now, there are some implications of this spiritual nature of the kingdom. Because of the spiritual nature of the kingdom, we can say that Jesus' kingdom is eternal and for all people for all time. The kingdom of heaven, which Jesus was introducing into the world, was not a physical city with literal streets of gold; neither was it a reference to heaven, where people might go after they die. Instead, the kingdom of heaven was something people could be a part of then and there in Jesus' day, because it had to do with how people think in their minds, or in other words, with states of heart. Also, if the kingdom of God is spiritual, then we should see the term as a metaphor. Actually, everything in God's revelation to humans is analogical. It has to be. How else could a transcendent God communicate heavenly concepts to earthbound humans (cf. John 3.1-15)? In the Sermon on the Mount, which we shall take up a little later, Jesus referred to kingdom people as "the light of the world. A city set on a hill cannot be hidden" (Matthew 5.14). In the Parable of the Talents (Matthew 25.14-30), the king returns and orders, "Cast the worthless servant into the outer darkness. In that place there will be weeping and gnashing of teeth" (cf. Matthew 8.12, 22.13). Spiritually, the kingdom of God is a brightly lit castle, sitting on top of a hill, offering eternal security to all who enter its gates, while outside in the darkness, those who failed to enter it will agonize in disappointment. Another implication is that, unlike earthly, human kingdoms, which always fall into decline and dissolution, Jesus' kingdom, being spiritual in nature, is not subject to the forces of deterioration. Remember what Gabriel told the young Mary:

> Do not be afraid, Mary, for you have found favor with God. And behold, you will conceive in your womb and bear a son, and you shall call his name Jesus. He will be great and will be called the Son of the Most High. And the Lord God will give to him the throne of his father David, and he will reign over the house of Jacob forever, and of his kingdom there will be no end.

We're trying to show why the kingdom should be the paradigm for applying the Bible to our lives. So far we've shown that Jesus' mission was to set up a spiritual kingdom. Understanding the spiritual nature of the kingdom is so critical, but there are other equally important attributes.

The Kingdom is Universal

One of the most precious aspects of the spiritual kingdom of Jesus is its universality. It's open to everyone in every culture, in every place, for all time. We shall see this in the following passages.

Matthew's gospel revolves around five lengthy speeches from his lips. These discourses in fact set out what Matthew wants to say are the most important things about Jesus. All five of them are about the kingdom. One of them consists of the Parables of the Kingdom (Matthew 13), mentioned above. Here is the Parable of the Mustard Seed (Matthew 13.31-32; cf. Mark 4.30-32 and Luke 13.18-19):

> The kingdom of heaven is like a grain of mustard seed that a man took and sowed in his field. It is the smallest of all seeds, but when it has grown it is larger than all the garden plants and becomes a tree, so that the

birds of the air come and make nests in its branches.
Jesus saw the kingdom starting out very small and eventually becoming very big and knew that his first disciples would need to be patient and not get discouraged at the early stages of the kingdom.

Another parable, similar to that, has to do with the kingdom being like leaven (Matthew 13.33; cf. Luke 13.20-21): "The kingdom of heaven is like leaven that a woman took and hid in three measures of flour, till it was all leavened." The point, of course, is that the kingdom was by its very nature intended to permeate the world.

Moving on from the Parables of the Kingdom, we can see the intended universality of the kingdom in some of the episodes of Jesus' ministry. Jesus struggled against the sense of entitlement which the Jews of his day had developed, probably as a result of their being oppressed so long, and this became a stumbling block to his message of universal accessibility to the kingdom of God. In Matthew 8.5-13 (comp. Luke 13.28-30) a Roman centurion showed great faith in Jesus by recognizing Jesus' authority to dismiss evil spirits at will:

> When he had entered Capernaum, a centurion came forward to him, appealing to him, "Lord, my servant is lying paralyzed at home, suffering terribly." And he said to him, "I will come and heal him." But the centurion replied, "Lord, I am not worthy to have you come under my roof, but only say the word, and my servant will be healed. For I too am a man under authority, with soldiers under me. And I say to one, 'Go,' and he goes, and to another, 'Come,' and he comes, and to my servant, 'Do this,' and he does it." When Jesus heard this, he marveled and said to those who followed him, "Truly, I tell you, with no one in Israel have I found such faith. I tell you, many will come from east and west and recline at table with Abraham, Isaac, and Jacob in the kingdom of heaven, while the sons of the kingdom will be thrown into the outer darkness. In that place there will be weeping and gnashing of teeth." And to the centurion Jesus said, "Go; let it be done for you as you have believed."
> And the servant was healed at that very moment.

The centurion's faith was evidenced by his respect for Jesus' authority.

Many of the Jews in Jesus' day rejected Jesus' authority; they did not regard him as the Messiah. Jesus was saying that in this kingdom he was setting up he anticipated Gentiles entering the kingdom, while "the sons of the kingdom", meaning the Jews, would reject his authority.

And though it's not so unusual to us today in the West, Jesus actually had women join his troop of disciples, as they went through cities and villages, preaching the good news of the kingdom of God (Luke 8.1-3). Not race, not nationality, not gender mattered.

Then there's the exchange around the Parable of the Wicked Tenants, which Jesus told during the last eleven days of his ministry (Matthew 21.33-46; cf. Mark 12.1-12 and Luke 20.9-19). Jesus said:

There was a master of a house who planted a vineyard and put a fence around it and dug a winepress in it and built a tower and leased it to tenants, and went into another country. When the season for fruit drew near, he sent his servants to the tenants to get his fruit. And the tenants took his servants and beat one, killed another, and stoned another. Again he sent other servants, more than the first. And they did the same to them. Finally he sent his son to them, saying, "They will respect my son." But when the tenants saw the son, they said to themselves, "This is the heir. Come, let us kill him and have his inheritance." And they took him and threw him out of the vineyard and killed him. When therefore the owner of the vineyard comes, what will he do to those tenants? They said to him, "He will put those wretches to a miserable death and let out the vineyard to other tenants who will give him the fruits in their seasons."

Jesus said to them, "Have you never read in the Scriptures:

The stone that the builders rejected
has become the cornerstone;
this was the Lord's doing,
and it is marvelous in our eyes?

Therefore I tell you, the kingdom of God will be taken away from you and given to a people producing its fruits. And the one who falls on this stone will be broken

to pieces; and when it falls on anyone, it will crush him."
The servants are God's prophets of old, while the tenants are the Jews.
The Jews had a record of rejecting God's prophets, and Jesus knew they
would reject him too. As a result, Jesus would open the gates of the
kingdom to anyone who would listen to God's prophets and obey them.

Another such parable of the kingdom follows immediately in
Matthew's account (22.1-14):

> The kingdom of heaven may be compared to a
> king who gave a wedding feast for his son, and sent his
> servants to call those who were invited to the wedding
> feast, but they would not come. Again he sent other ser-
> vants, saying, "Tell those who are invited, 'See, I have
> prepared my dinner, my oxen and my fat calves have
> been slaughtered, and everything is ready. Come to the
> wedding feast'" But they paid no attention and went off,
> one to his farm, another to his business, while the rest
> seized his servants, treated them shamefully, and killed
> them. The king was angry, and he sent his troops and
> destroyed those murderers and burned their city. Then
> he said to his servants, "The wedding feast is ready,
> but those invited were not worthy. Go therefore to the
> main roads and invite to the wedding feast as many as
> you find." And those servants went out into the roads
> and gathered all whom they found, both bad and good.
> So the wedding hall was filled with guests. But when
> the king came in to look at the guests, he saw there a
> man who had no wedding garment. And he said to him,
> "Friend, how did you get in here without a wedding gar-
> ment?" And he was speechless. Then the king said to
> the attendants, "Bind him hand and foot and cast him
> into the outer darkness. In that place here will be weep-
> ing and gnashing of teeth. For many are called, but few
> are chosen."

The point of the parable is that all are invited into the kingdom, whether
Jew or Gentile, whether high or low, though whoever would desire to
enter Jesus' kingdom must have a grateful and respectful attitude toward
the king.

Finally, Jesus declared in his Olivet Discourse his intention that "this gospel of the kingdom will be proclaimed throughout the whole world as a testimony to all nations" (Matthew 24.14).

The Imminence of the Kingdom

We, of course, shouldn't be hard on Jesus' audience. Today we have the advantage of seeing the spiritual nature of the kingdom more clearly, especially once we recognize that the kingdom was presented by John, Jesus and Jesus' immediate disciples as imminent (Matthew 3.1-2, 4.17, 10.7, Luke 10.9). Therefore, we want at this point to review several events and teachings in the gospels which bolster their claim that the kingdom of heaven was "at hand". There are several of them, so we shall review them in rather quick order. But the point is that if the kingdom was imminent to them and no earthly kingdom ever got set up, then it would follow that it was a spiritual kingdom. We can see that now, even though it was difficult for the people in Jesus' day to see it. So, let's look at how much emphasis was placed on the imminence of the kingdom.

As we saw in the Beelzebul episode, Jesus said to the people of his day that the miracles performed by him through the Holy Spirit were evidence that the kingdom of God had come upon them (Matthew 12.28, Luke 11.20).

After the Feeding of the Five Thousand and most of Jesus' disciples had abandoned him, a frustrated Jesus pulled his immediate disciples aside to discuss his mission with them (Matthew 16.13-23; cf. Mark 8.27-33, Luke 9.18-22):

> Now when Jesus came into the district of Caesarea Philippi, he asked his disciples, "Who do people say that the Son of Man is?" And they said, "Some say John the Baptist, others say Elijah, and others Jeremiah or one of the prophets." He said to them, "But who do you say that I am?" Simon Peter replied, "You are the Christ, the Son of the living God." And Jesus answered him, "Blessed are you, Simon Bar-Jonah! For flesh and blood has not revealed this to you, but my Father who is in heaven. And I tell you, you are Peter, and on this rock

I will build my church, and the gates of hell shall not prevail against it. I will give you the keys of the kingdom of heaven, and whatever you bind on earth shall be bound in heaven, and whatever you loose on earth shall be loosed in heaven." Then he strictly charged the disciples to tell no one that he was the Christ.

From that time Jesus began to show his disciples that he must go to Jerusalem and suffer many things from the elders and chief priests and scribes, and be killed, and on the third day be raised. And Peter took him aside and began to rebuke him, saying, "Far be it from you, Lord! This shall never happen to you." But he turned and said to Peter, "Get behind me, Satan! You are a hindrance to me. For you are not setting your mind on the things of God, but on the things of man."

Then Jesus told his disciples, "If anyone would come after me, let him deny himself and take up his cross and follow me. For whoever would save his life will lose it, but whoever loses his life for my sake will find it. For what will it profit a man if he gains the whole world and forfeits his soul? Or what shall a man give in return for his soul? For the Son of Man is going to come with his angels in the glory of his Father, and then he will repay each person according to what he has done. Truly, I say to you, there are some standing here who will not taste death until they see the Son of Man coming in his kingdom."

This is a very important kingdom passage, which speaks to how the people were unable to grasp the nature of Jesus' kingdom, including one of Jesus' own disciples, because it required a completely new and different way of thinking.[6]

From Matthew's third discourse, the Parables of the Kingdom again, comes the Parable of the Weeds (Matthew 13.24-30):

---

6 In this passage, we also see the spiritual nature of the kingdom emphasized again. Conspicuously absent from the people's answers to Jesus' question was that he was the Messiah, because they saw the kingdom in human terms. But Peter held out for Jesus being the Messiah. As a result, in the middle of this discussion, Jesus gave Peter a new

The kingdom of heaven may be compared to a man who sowed good seed in his field, but while his men were sleeping, his enemy came and sowed weeds among the wheat and went away. So when the plants came up and bore grain, then the weeds appeared also. And the servants of the master of the house came and said to him, "Master, did you not sow good seed in your field? How then does it have weeds?" He said to them, "An enemy has done this." So the servants said to him, "Then do you want us to go and gather them?" But he said, "No, lest in gathering the weeds you root up the wheat along with them. Let both grow together until the harvest, and at harvest time I will tell the reapers, 'Gather the weeds first and bind them in bundles to be burned, but gather the wheat into my barn.'"

And its interpretation by Jesus himself (13.36-43):

The one who sows the good seed is the Son of Man. The field is the world, and the good seed is the sons of the kingdom. The weeds are the sons of the evil one, and the enemy who sowed them is the devil. The harvest is the end of the age, and the reapers are angels. Just as the weeds are gathered and burned with fire, so will it be at the end of the age. The Son of Man will send his angels, and they will gather out of his kingdom all causes of sin and all law-breakers, and throw them into the fiery furnace. In that place there will be weeping

---

name. Most commentators note that the word "Peter" means rock and that Jesus is giving Peter this new name because of his confession he just made about the messiahship of Jesus. It is possible, though, that the rock that Jesus is talking about is Peter's insight that the kingdom is spiritual instead of fleshly. Peter was different from the crowds, which had often heard Jesus, in that he could catch a glimpse of the spiritual nature of the kingdom instead of seeing Jesus as a human king, ruling a human kingdom in the physical world. This is amplified later when Peter rebuked Jesus for making his prediction that he would be killed by the Jewish leaders in Jerusalem. But Jesus responded to Peter's rebuke by saying that he, Peter, had now gone over to the side of men. Perhaps it is not Peter who is the rock on which the church is built, neither is it faith in Jesus as Messiah, but yet something more fundamental, namely, that the kingdom would be a spiritual one, not human and not fleshly.

> and gnashing of teeth. Then the righteous will shine like
> the sun in the kingdom of their Father. He who has
> ears, let him hear.

Though the imminence factor is not as clear in this passage as in others, it appears that Jesus saw himself at a phase in the kingdom of heaven where God would be sorting out the good from the bad, a phase in fact called "the end of the age". (We think the fiery furnace refers to the destruction of city of Jerusalem, which occurred in AD 70, but a discussion of that is outside the purview of this book.) In this parable, "the sons of the kingdom" appear to be righteous Jews. Righteous, lawful, Jews, therefore, would achieve kingdom citizenship. Jesus' last phrase, about hearing, shows how different his view of the kingdom was and how the listener would be required to think of the kingdom according to a new and revolutionary paradigm.

Similarly, there is the parable of the net (13.47-50):

> Again, the kingdom of heaven is like a net that
> was thrown into the sea and gathered fish of every kind.
> When it was full, men drew it ashore and sat down and
> sorted the good into containers but threw away the bad.
> So it will be at the end of the age. The angels will come
> out and separate the evil from the righteous and throw
> them into the fiery furnace. In that place there will be
> weeping and gnashing of teeth.

Jesus predicted his return several times. The most famous prediction is found in Matthew's Fifth Discourse, which we call the "Olivet Discourse" (Matthew 24.4-25.46; cf. Mark 13.5-37, Luke 21.8-36), where Jesus predicted a period of great stress and false messiahs, during which "this gospel of the kingdom will be proclaimed throughout the whole world as a testimony to all nations" (Matthew 24.14). Then would come the end, Jesus predicted, when he would return "with power and great glory" (Matthew 24.30; cf. Mark 13.26, Luke 21.27). We recognize that our view on this is very controversial, but from the description of things in the Olivet Discourse we believe he was talking about the fall of Jerusalem, which occurred in AD 70. At any rate, Luke elsewhere uses the same language as the Olivet Discourse and calls it the coming of the kingdom of God (Luke 17.20-37). Notice especially vv.20-21: "Being asked by the Pharisees when the kingdom of God would come, he answered them, 'The kingdom of God is not coming in ways that can be observed, nor will they say, "Look, here it is!" or "There!" for behold, the kingdom of God is in the midst of you.'" In other words, it would be, not a physically observable event, but rather a spiritual one. The fall of Jerusalem would therefore be a sign that Jesus had spiritually returned as king over his spiritual kingdom. Notice what all three synoptic gospel writers record from the words of Jesus (Luke 21.29-32; cf. Matthew 24.32-34, Mark 13.28-30):

> And he told them a parable: "Look at the fig tree, and all the trees. As soon as they come out in leaf, you see for yourselves and know that the summer is already near. So also, when you see these things taking place, you know that the kingdom of God is near. Truly, I say to you, this generation will not pass away until all has taken place."

In fact, Luke describes the end of the Jewish age and the coming of the Messiah's kingdom in the following way (Luke 21.20), "But when you see Jerusalem surrounded by armies, then know that its desolation has come near."

Jesus concluded the discourse with three parables about the kingdom. The first of these (25.1-13) is the parable of the ten bridesmaids:

> Then the kingdom of heaven will be like ten virgins who took their lamps and went to meet the bridegroom. Five of them were foolish, and five were wise. For when the foolish took their lamps, they took no oil with them, but the wise took flasks of oil with their lamps. As the bridegroom was delayed, they all became drowsy and slept. But at midnight there was a cry, "Here is the bridegroom! Come out to meet him." Then all those virgins rose and trimmed their lamps. And the foolish said to the wise, "Give us some of your oil, for our lamps are going out." But the wise answered, saying, "Since there will not be enough for us and for you, go rather to the dealers and buy for yourselves." And while they were going to buy, the bridegroom came, and those who were ready went in with him to the marriage

feast, and the door was shut. Afterward the other virgins came also, saying, "Lord, lord, open to us." But he answered, "Truly, I say to you, I do not know you." Watch therefore, for you know neither the day nor the hour.

The point of the parable is that Jesus' disciples should be ready for his return to set up the kingdom. Again, one of the things made clear in the gospels was that the coming of the kingdom of the Messiah was imminent.

The third of these kingdom parables is found in 25.31-46. Jesus as Messiah is sitting on his throne and making a judgment between the sheep and the goats:

When the Son of Man comes in his glory, and all the angels with him, then he will sit on his glorious throne. Before him will be gathered all the nations, and he will separate people one from another as a shepherd separates the sheep from the goats. And he will place the sheep on his right, but the goats on the left. Then the King will say to those on his right, "Come, you who are blessed by my Father, inherit the kingdom prepared for you from the foundation of the world. For I was hungry and you gave me food, I was thirsty and you gave me drink, I was a stranger and you welcomed me, I was naked and you clothed me, I was sick and you visited me, I was in prison and you came to me." Then the righteous will answer him, saying, "Lord, when did we see you hungry and feed you, or thirsty and give you drink? And when did we see you a stranger and welcome you, or naked and clothe you? And when did we see you sick or in prison and visit you?" And the King will answer them, "Truly, I say to you, as you did it to one of the least of these my brothers, you did it to me."

Then he will say to those on his left, "Depart from me, you cursed, into the eternal fire prepared for the devil and his angels. For I was hungry and you gave me no food, I was thirsty and you gave me no drink, I was a stranger and you did not welcome me, naked and you did not clothe me, sick and in prison and you did not visit me." Then they also will answer, saying, "Lord, when did we see you hungry or thirsty or a stranger or naked or sick or in prison, and did not minister to you?" Then he will answer them, saying, "Truly, I say to you, as you did not do it to one of the least of these, you did not do it to me." And these will go away into eternal punishment, but the righteous into eternal life.

Jesus as "the King" invites into his kingdom those righteous people who had served Jesus' disciples ("my brothers") when they were persecuted. Those righteous people would not only enter the kingdom, but there they would also find eternal life. Jesus predicted that, as the gospel would spread outside the bounds of Jewry, that the Gentiles would see his disciples suffering and then some would help them, ostensibly becoming disciples themselves. They would enter the kingdom and there find eternal life. This is not a passage about social activism but about being able to see the hand of God in the persecutions of Christians and appropriately responding. Notice also the statement that Jesus' kingdom had been foreordained from creation.

So, in conclusion, it is important to understand that the kingdom of heaven, about which John and Jesus were preaching, was not heaven and was not something that was coming in their distant future but was instead the newest installment of God's program for this world. It was "at hand", it was being established by John and Jesus, and there were things that people could do immediately to enter the kingdom.

Twelve Thrones

We should also note that Jesus selected twelve special disciples who were to play a special role in his forthcoming kingdom. Jesus promised the Twelve that they would sit on twelve thrones, judging the twelve tribes of Israel (Matthew 19.28). At the Last Supper, Jesus said to his disciples, "You are those who have stayed with me in my trials, and I assign to you, as my Father assigned to me, a kingdom, that you may eat and drink at my table in my kingdom and sit on thrones judging the twelve tribes of Israel" (Luke 22.28-30). As we saw in Matthew 16 above, Jesus responded to Peter's answer by promising him authority in the kingdom. But it is also very important at this point to notice Matthew 18.18-19, which applies that same language to all of the apostles; this promise of authority was made to all of the Twelve. So, we take this to mean that the Twelve were a select group of people who would hammer out the details of Jesus' kingdom after Jesus' ascension to the father. A great deal more could be said about the Twelve, but at this point suffice it to say that they had a special role in the kingdom of God: they would oversee its early development, and they would implement the principles of the kingdom.

Conclusion

When one takes the scriptures seriously he sees that God had an eternal plan for the ages which culminated in the mission of Jesus, the Messiah. Jesus' aim was to set up an eternal, spiritual kingdom for all people and all cultures. That kingdom affords people salvation from the judgment of God and eternal life with God in heaven. This is the center of the gospel, which fact supports our thesis that the way we, as modern day followers of Christ, are to read the Bible involves first finding and applying those passages which deal with the kingdom of God and to view them as universally binding (we will discuss the relevance of the rest of the scriptures later). But now, let's go back to the gospels to find out just what those universal kingdom teachings might be.

4 The Kingdom Essentials

We propose that whatever one finds in the Bible as inextricably essential to the spiritual kingdom of Christ be obligatory for all Christians for all time; otherwise not. This is our algorithm. In this chapter, we want to take up where we left off, namely, the gospels. We want to comb more kingdom passages in the accounts of Jesus' mission to get a picture of what kingdom citizenship entails.

A Central Story and Parable

We go to the story of the rich young man who came to Jesus to inquire about eternal life (Matthew 19.16-30; cf. Mark 10.17-31, Luke 18.18-30). It will become clearer as we go along why this section of the gospel is so important:

> And behold, a man came up to him, saying, "Teacher, what good deed must I do to have eternal life?" And he said to him, "Why do you ask me about what is good? There is only one who is good. If you would enter life, keep the commandments." He said to him, "Which ones?" And Jesus said, "You shall not mur-

der, You shall not commit adultery, You shall not steal, You shall not bear false witness, Honor your father and mother, and, You shall love your neighbor as yourself." The young man said to him, "All these I have kept. What do I still lack?" Jesus said to him, "If you would be perfect, go, sell what you possess and give to the poor, and you will have treasure in heaven; and come, follow me." When the young man heard this he went away sorrowful, for he had great possessions.

And Jesus said to his disciples, "Truly, I say to you, only with difficulty will a rich person enter the kingdom of heaven. Again I tell you, it is easier for a camel to go through the eye of a needle than for a rich person to enter the kingdom of God." When the disciples heard this, they were greatly astonished, saying, "Who then can be saved?" But Jesus looked at them and said, "With man this is impossible, but with God all things are possible." Then Peter said in reply, "See, we have left everything and followed you. What then will we have?" Jesus said to them, "Truly, I say to you, in the new world, when the Son of Man will sit on his glorious throne, you who have followed me will also sit on twelve thrones, judging the twelve tribes of Israel. And everyone who has left houses or brothers or sisters or father or mother or children or lands, for my name's sake, will receive a hundredfold and will inherit eternal life. But many who are first will be last, and the last first.

There are several insights into the kingdom which we can gain from the exchange between Jesus and the rich young man. The first insight is that terms such as "eternal life", "life", "having treasure in heaven", "entering the kingdom of heaven", "entering the kingdom of God" and "being saved" are interchangeable. Perhaps we should say that they are virtually interchangeable, since there are nuances that belong to each one of these terms which might not belong to others on the list. But we can say at this point that citizenship in the kingdom would bring one eternal life, heavenly treasures, and salvation.

A second point would be the following. Though we can tell

from the later history of Christians as found in the Book of Acts and in the epistles that it was not required of all disciples to sell all of their wealth, we can still say that Jesus wanted this young man to do so. The principle seems to be this: wealth can be a hindrance to a person's entering the kingdom. It should be expected that life in the eternal, spiritual kingdom of Christ will cost the disciple materially on some level. That's what the disciples found so amazing.

However, this does raise a question about the algorithm, namely, why should not selling all of one's possession and giving the proceeds to the poor be a kingdom demand of all of its citizens, for all times and for all places? Does this not reflect a fallacy in the algorithm? But this is one of the reasons we chose to highlight this story. Jesus does make the demand of that young man. Jesus does lay great stress on the kingdom of heaven in this story. But nowhere in the story do we find Jesus explicitly saying that in order to enter the kingdom one must sell his possessions. The story is illustrative of some very important principles, but that explicit condition is not set forth. And that's our point. We're saying that the modern day disciple should read her Bible, looking for those explicit conditions of the kingdom. There are other reasons for her to read her Bible, but the explicit kingdom requirements are all that are universally obligatory.

Thirdly, we see again the spiritual nature of Jesus' kingdom. The problem with the young man was that he was in love with the flesh, so much so that he could not turn it loose to become an immediate follower of Jesus. In 19.28 Jesus referred to his kingdom as the new world. The NIV has "the future world". But both the KJV and the NASV follow the Greek more closely and use the word "regeneration". Our point here is that Jesus' kingdom was going to be so radically new and different that he could even speak of the world as being reborn. Where the age of Moses' law was physical, the new age would be spiritual. And that is where the rich young man had problems.

Lastly, just as we saw in Matthew 18, these twelve disciples of Jesus were to have a special role in the kingdom; they would sit on twelve thrones and serve as judges. Once again, the Twelve need to be recognized as having a special role in hammering out the details of the kingdom.

Jesus finished his discussion with the disciples after the departure of the rich young man by saying, "But any that are first shall be last, and last first." Jesus immediately explained this concluding statement by offering another of his famous kingdom parables, found only in the Gospel of Matthew (20.1-16):

> For the kingdom of heaven is like a master of a house who went out early in the morning to hire laborers for his vineyard. After agreeing with the laborers for a denarius a day, he sent them into his vineyard. And going out about the third hour he saw others standing idle in the marketplace, and to them he said, "You go into the vineyard too, and whatever is right I will give you." So they went. Going out again about the sixth hour and the ninth hour, he did the same. And about the eleventh hour he went out and found others standing. And he said to them, "Why do you stand here idle all day?" They said to him, "Because no one has hired us." He said to them, "You go into the vineyard too." And when evening came, the owner of the vineyard said to his foreman, "Call the laborers and pay them their wages, beginning with the last, up to the first." And when those hired about the eleventh hour came, each of them received a denarius. Now when those hired first came, they thought they would receive more, but each of them also received a denarius. And on receiving it they grumbled at the master of the house, saying, "These last worked only one hour, and you have made them equal to us who have borne the burden of the day and the scorching heat." But he replied to one of them, "Friend, I am doing you no wrong. Did you not agree with me for a denarius? Take what belongs to you and go. I choose to give to this last worker as I give to you. Am I not allowed to do what I choose with what belongs to me? Or do you begrudge my generosity?" So the last will be first, and the first last.

The parable begins with "For", showing its connection with the story of the rich young man. Jesus also ends the parable with the phrase, "So the last will be first, and the first last", which is how he ended his comments with the disciples. This parable is not about heaven, rather it's about

Jesus' spiritual kingdom. The main point of the parable is how generous God is. As was characteristic of most of Jesus' recorded parables, there is a surprising twist to the storyline. Whereas a typical Jewish audience would have expected different pay for different amounts of work, in Jesus' parable all the workers were paid the same. This is why the first workers grumbled and the master had to inquire as to whether they thought he had done them wrong. In this parable, the vineyard is the kingdom (cf. Isaiah 5.1-7, as well as others of Jesus' parables), and the first workers are Jesus' immediate group of disciples who think they have a leg up on getting into the Messiah's kingdom.

The parable is framed, on the one side, by Peter's question, "What then shall we have?", and on the other side, by the request of the mother of James and John, which we shall take up next (Matthew 20.20-28; cf. Mark 10.35-45):

> Then the mother of the sons of Zebedee came up to him with her sons, and kneeling before him she asked him for something. And he said to her, "What do you want?" She said to him, "Say that these two sons of mine are to sit, one at your right hand and one at your left, in your kingdom." Jesus answered, "You do not know what you are asking. Are you able to drink the cup that I am to drink?" They said to him, "We are able." He said to them, "You will drink my cup, but to sit at my right hand and at my left is not mine to grant, but it is for those for whom it has been prepared by my Father." And when the ten heard it, they were indignant at the two brothers. But Jesus called them to him and said, "You know that the rulers of the Gentiles lord it over them, and their great ones exercise authority over them. It shall not be so among you. But whoever would be great among you must be your servant, and whoever would be first among you must be your slave, even as the Son of Man came not to be served but to serve, and to give his life as a ransom for many."

We take this whole episode, along with Matthew's framing and the parable, to mean that the spiritual nature of Jesus' kingdom is so transcendently wonderful that it renders all the human and physical circumstances of this life irrelevant. Jesus was telling his disciples that it did not matter what they had had to sacrifice or what they had suffered; in comparison to their roles in the upcoming kingdom, these deprivations would be insignificant. Once again, Jesus saw his kingdom as the overarching purpose of his mission.

Speaking of sacrifice, all three of the synoptic accounts have Jesus continuing to lead his disciples on his mission of death in Jerusalem. He reminded them that instead of setting up an earthly kingdom with him being a physical king sitting on a material throne, that he was about to be killed by his Jewish opponents in Jerusalem, that they would persecute him and then deliver him to the Gentiles to be crucified. Incredibly, instead of his disciples grasping the spiritual nature of his kingdom, two of them, James and John, along with their mother appealed to Jesus for positions of authority in his upcoming kingdom (Matthew 20.20-28, Mark 10.35-45). When the mother of the sons of Zebedee asked for these positions, it betrayed a view on her part that the kingdom would be earthly and political. It was as if she were asking that her two sons be awarded the positions of Secretary of State and Secretary of Defense, respectively. Jesus answered her, "You do not know what you are asking." He said that he had a cup for them to drink but it might not be glorious positions of human authority. And neither were the other ten disciples in any sort of position superior to the two, because they were indignant at James and John, whom they saw as attempting to co-opt authority in the kingdom. Also, Jesus' response about Gentile rulers was very telling. One of the essential characteristics of Jesus' kingdom would be a heart of servanthood rather than a desire to grasp power and control.[1]

We started out with an examination of the rich young ruler episode, because we think it boldly reflects so many themes having to do with the kingdom of God. In the rest of this chapter, we want to set out in an orderly way what the kingdom essentials are. In other words, we will outline what The Kingdom Algorithm yields as what God wants of all Christ followers, for all times, in all places and in all cultures.

---

1 Incidentally, an example of the "last" could very well be Bartimaeus, who immediately followed Jesus into Jerusalem (Matthew 20.34, Mark 10.52 and Luke 18.43), while Jesus' main disciples were reticent (Matthew 16.22, 17.22-23, 20.17-19, Mark 8.32, 9.30-32, 10.32-34 and Luke 9.43b-45).

Kingdom First

One of the principles which emerges from the story of the rich young man is the value of the kingdom of God. For followers of Christ, the kingdom must come first. Jesus said in Matthew 6.33, "But seek first the kingdom of God and his righteousness, and all these things will be added to you." Once again, we find Jesus saying that the kingdom of God is not about food, drink, or clothing, but about righteousness. The citizen of Jesus' eternal spiritual kingdom would be someone who placed righteousness above all physical things. Similarly, there are the parables of the hidden treasure and the precious pearl (Matthew 13.44-46):

> The kingdom of heaven is like treasure hidden in a field, which a man found and covered up. Then in his joy he goes and sells all that he has and buys that field.
> Again, the kingdom of heaven is like a merchant in search of fine pearls, who, on finding one pearl of great value, went and sold all that he had and bought it.

The matter of priorities comes up again in Matthew 19.3-12 (cf. Mark 10.2-12):

> And Pharisees came up to him and tested him by asking, "Is it lawful to divorce one's wife for any cause?" He answered, "Have you not read that he who created them from the beginning made them male and female, and said, 'Therefore a man shall leave his father and his mother and hold fast to his wife, and the two shall become one flesh'? So they are no longer two but one flesh. What therefore God has joined together, let not man separate." They said to him, "Why then did Moses command one to give a certificate of divorce and to send her away?" He said to them, "Because of your hardness of heart Moses allowed you to divorce your wives, but from the beginning it was not so. And I say to you: whoever divorces his wife, except for sexual immorality, and marries another, commits adultery. The disciples said to him, "If such is the case of a man with his wife, it is better not to marry." But he said to them, "Not everyone

can receive this saying, but only those to whom it is giv-
en. For there are eunuchs who have been so from birth,
and there are eunuchs who have been made eunuchs by
men, and there are eunuchs who have made themselves
eunuchs for the sake of the kingdom of heaven. Let the
one who is able to receive this receive it."

Jesus held a very stringent view on divorce and remarrying, one which
his own disciples found shocking. They responded, in fact, to his views
by suggesting that their master's stringency might mean that it would
be best for a man not even to marry at all. It is at this point that Jesus
makes the memorable statement that some have made themselves eunuchs for the kingdom of heaven. The divorce issue has been interpreted along a wide range of possibilities, and this is not the place to go
into them here, but marriage and divorce are kingdom issues. However,
for our purposes, Jesus' point seems to be that the kingdom of heaven
trumps all fleshly concerns, even marriage. His remarks fly in the face
of the current American obsession with happiness, especially marital
and sexual happiness.

Obedience to King Jesus

The very idea of a kingdom is that there is a king and his subjects must obey him. This was the point about the centurion in Matthew
8.5-13. As a Roman soldier, he recognized authority. So, if one were to
place the kingdom at the top of his life's priorities, he would be committing himself to obedience. In the Lord's Prayer we find the typical Jewish doublet (Matthew 6.10), "Your kingdom come, your will be done, on
earth as it is in heaven." People doing God's will on earth is equivalent
to God's kingdom having come to earth. Jesus also said (Matthew 7.21-
23):

"Not everyone who says to me, 'Lord, Lord,'
will enter the kingdom of heaven, but the one who does
the will of my Father who is in heaven. On that day many
will say to me, 'Lord, Lord, did we not prophesy in your
name, and cast out demons in your name, and do many
mighty works in your name?' And then will I declare to
them, 'I never knew you; depart from me, you workers

of lawlessness.'"

Obedience to God's will, therefore, trumps everything else, even casting out demons. From the Parable of the Wicked Tenants (Matthew 21.33-46), which we examined above, we see that the kingdom would be taken away from the wicked and given to those bearing fruit.

Luke's version of the Parable of the Talents (Luke 19.12-27) goes like this:

> A nobleman went into a far country to receive for himself a kingdom and then return. Calling ten of his servants, he gave them ten minas, and said to them, "Engage in business until I come." But his citizens hated him and sent a delegation after him, saying, "We do not want this man to reign over us." When he returned, having received the kingdom, he ordered these servants to whom he had given the money to be called to him, that he might know what they had gained by doing business. The first came before him, saying, "Lord, your mina has made ten minas more." And he said to him, 'Well done, good servant! Because you have been faithful in a very little, you shall have authority over ten cities." And the second came, saying, "Lord, your mina has made five minas." And he said to him, "And you are to be over five cities." Then another came, saying, "Lord, here is your mina, which I kept laid away in a handkerchief; for I was afraid of you, because you are a severe man. You take what you did not deposit, and reap what you did not sow." He said to him, "I will condemn you with your own words, you wicked servant! You knew that I was a severe man, taking what I did not deposit and reaping what I did not sow? Why then did you not put my money in the bank, and at my coming I might have collected it with interest?" And he said to those who stood by, "Take the mina from him, and give it to the one who has the ten minas." And they said to him, "Lord, he has ten minas!" I tell you that to everyone who has, more will be given, but from the one who has not, even what he has will be taken away. But as for these enemies of mine, who did

not want me to reign over them, bring them here and
slaughter them before me.'

The parable is brutal, but the point is unmistakable. If we understand
earthly kings, then we should understand that King Jesus requires submission and initiative.

The Basic Principles of the Kingdom

Obedience to King Jesus starts with certain basics. As we said
above, the Gospel of Matthew is organized around five great discourses.
The greatest and the most famous of these is what we call today the Sermon on the Mount (Matthew 5-7), which is about the basic principles of
the kingdom. It opens in the following way.

Seeing the crowds, he went up on the mountain,
and when he sat down, his disciples came to him. And
he opened his mouth and taught them, saying:

"Blessed are the poor in spirit, for theirs is the
kingdom of heaven.

Blessed are those who mourn, for they shall
be comforted.

Blessed are the meek, for they shall inherit
the earth.

Blessed are those who hunger and thirst for righteousness, for they shall be satisfied.

Blessed are the merciful, for they shall receive mercy.

Blessed are the pure in heart, for they shall
see God.

Blessed are the peacemakers, for they shall be
called sons of God.

Blessed are those who are persecuted for righteousness' sake, for theirs is the kingdom of heaven.

Blessed are you when others revile you and persecute you and utter all kinds of evil against you falsely
on my account. Rejoice and be glad, for your reward is
great in heaven, for so they persecuted the prophets who
were before you.

You are the salt of the earth, but if salt has lost its taste, how shall its saltiness be restored? It is no longer good for anything except to be thrown out and trampled under people's feet.

You are the light of the world. A city set on a hill cannot be hidden. Nor do people light a lamp and put it under a basket, but on a stand, and it gives light to all in the house. In the same way, let your light shine before others, so that they may see your good works and give glory to your Father who is in heaven.

Do not think that I have come to abolish the Law or the Prophets; I have not come to abolish them but to fulfill them. For truly, I say to you, until heaven and earth pass away, not an iota, not a dot, will pass from the Law until all is accomplished. Therefore whoever relaxes one of the least of these commandments and teaches others to do the same will be called least in the kingdom of heaven, but whoever does them and teaches them will be called great in the kingdom of heaven. For I tell you, unless your righteousness exceeds that of the scribes and Pharisees, you will never enter the kingdom of heaven."

The first one of the Beatitudes, "Blessed are the poor in spirit for theirs is the kingdom of heaven," and the last one, "Blessed are those who are persecuted for righteousness sake, for theirs is the kingdom of heaven," serve as bookends to show that all of this is really about the kingdom. In between are macarisms (blessings pronouncements) for states of heart such as serious repentance, meekness, hungering and thirsting for righteousness, mercifulness, purity of heart, and a desire for peace. These are the basic characteristics of citizens of Jesus' kingdom. As Matthew says in 4.23, Jesus went about all Galilee teaching in the synagogues and preaching the gospel of the kingdom, and Matthew then gives us the Sermon on the Mount to show us what the gospel of the kingdom was.

Later on in the Sermon on the Mount in 5.17-20, Jesus said that there are lesser and greater commandments in the kingdom. One might fail with regard to the lesser commandments but still be in the kingdom, but if one is like the scribes and Pharisees of Jesus' day, failing in the greater commandments, then they would not enter the kingdom. In Matthew 23, which is the flip side of the Sermon on the Mount, the scribes and Pharisees are described in very negative terms. From a comparison of Matthew 23, on the one hand, with the Sermon on the Mount, on the other, the reader can see that what constituted the essential nature of the kingdom of heaven was a state of heart, certain attitudes like humility and meekness, and that these attitudes were essential to the kingdom. In Matthew 23.23-24 Jesus said:

> Woe to you, scribes and Pharisees, hypocrites! For you tithe mint and dill and cumin, and have neglected the weightier matters of the law: justice and mercy and faithfulness. These you ought to have done, without neglecting the others. You blind guides, straining out a gnat and swallowing a camel!

Then again (Matthew 23.13):

> But woe to you, scribes and Pharisees, hypocrites! For you shut the kingdom of heaven in people's faces. For you neither enter yourselves nor allow those who would enter to go in.

Jesus' remarks, then, against the Pharisees constitute a reverse reflection of the essentials of the kingdom. In the Sermon on the Mount, Jesus explicitly used the Pharisees as his foil. So, his denunciation of the Pharisees in Matthew 23 sets forth the very things that would prevent someone from being a citizen in the kingdom. Matthew 23 very clearly describes what it was about the Pharisees that excluded them from the kingdom. In a word, it was hypocrisy. Hypocrisy is intentionally putting up a front of righteousness when in truth one is knowingly not living righteously. Jesus accused these Pharisees also of arrogance, of duplicity, of omitting justice, mercy and faith from their lives,[2] of extortion and abuse of vulnerable people. Clearly, those things were keeping them out of Jesus' kingdom.

The problem with the scribes and Pharisees of Jesus' day was

---

2 There is general scholarly agreement that Jesus is relying here on generally understood Old Testament virtues, which can be lifted from the prophets especially (Isaiah 1.17, Jeremiah 22.3, Hosea 6.6, Zechariah 7.9-10, Micah 6.8 and Habakkuk 2.4). Lesser commandments, for Jesus, included tithing, but greater elements of the law included justice, actively taking care of others who are in need, mercy, the general love that one should have for his neighbor, and faithfulness, trusting in God. See Donald A. Hagner, Matthew 14-28, *Word Biblical Commentary*, Vol. 33B, Nashville: Thomas Nelson, 1995, p. 670.

that they majored in the minor parts of God's law while omitting the major parts, attitudes of justice, mercy, and dependence upon God. It should be clear from a reading of the Sermon on the Mount that the essential characteristics of the kingdom have to do with godly attitudes.

Humility and Repentance

This brings us to one of the most often mentioned attitudes in connection with the kingdom, namely, humility. The fourth major discourse in the Gospel of Matthew (chapter 18) is devoted to the issue of humility and its ramifications. It starts like this (vv. 1-4; cf. Matthew 19.13-15, Mar 10.13-16, Luke18.15-17):

At that time the disciples came to Jesus, saying, "Who is the greatest in the kingdom of heaven?" And calling to him a child, he put him in the midst of them and said, "Truly, I say to you, unless you turn and become like children, you will never enter the kingdom of heaven. Whoever humbles himself like this child is the greatest in the kingdom of heaven."

Humility, therefore, is a necessary condition for citizenship in the Messiah's kingdom. In the rest of the chapter he brings up similar attitudes, such as being careful not to encourage sin in the lives of people around us (vs. 6). Similarly, in vv. 7-9 Jesus makes the point that a citizen in his kingdom would be willing to pay any price to stay out of sin. This leads to a discussion among Jesus and his disciples about forgiveness. In vv. 10-23 Jesus says that his followers should seek to be at peace with each other. And then in the last part of the discussion, Jesus tells the parable of the kingdom about a king who wishes to settle accounts with his servants (vv. 23-35):

Therefore the kingdom of heaven may be compared to a king who wished to settle accounts with his servants. When he began to settle, one was brought to him who owed him ten thousand talents. And since he could not pay, his master ordered him to be sold, with his wife and children and all that he had, and payment to be made. So the servant fell on his knees, imploring him, "Have patience with me, and I will pay you everything."

And out of pity for him, the master of that servant re-
leased him and forgave him the debt. But when that
same servant went out, he found one of his fellow servants who owed him a hundred denarii, and seizing him,
he began to choke him, saying, "Pay what you owe."
So his fellow servant fell down and pleaded with him,
"Have patience with me, and I will pay you." He refused and went and put him in prison until he should pay
the debt. When his fellow servants saw what had taken
place, they were greatly distressed, and they went and
reported to their master all that had taken place. Then
his master summoned him and said to him, "You wicked
servant! I forgave you all that debt because you pleaded
with me. And should not you have had mercy on your
fellow servant, as I had mercy on you?" And in anger
his master delivered him to the jailers, until he should
pay all his debt. So also my heavenly Father will do to
every one of you, if you do not forgive your brother
from your heart.

From this major discourse in Matthew's gospel we garner the following
conclusions about the essentials of Jesus' kingdom. Those who would
be a part of Jesus' kingdom must be humble, concerned about their
brothers and willing to forgive them.

All four gospel accounts make the last eleven days of Jesus'
ministry the most expansive part of their records. It begins with Jesus'
entry into Jerusalem (Matthew 21.1-9; Mark 11.1-10 Luke 19.28-38):

Now when they drew near to Jerusalem and came
to Bethphage, to the Mount of Olives, then Jesus sent
two disciples, saying to them, "Go into the village in
front of you, and immediately you will find a donkey
tied, and a colt with her. Untie them and bring them to
me. If anyone says anything to you, you shall say, 'The
Lord needs them,' and he will send them at once." This
took place to fulfill what was spoken by the
prophet, saying:

"Say to the daughter of Zion,

'Behold, your king is coming to you,

> humble, and mounted on a donkey,
> on a colt, the foal of a beast of burden.'"
> The disciples went and did as Jesus had directed them. They brought the donkey and the colt and put on them their cloaks, and he sat on them. Most of the crowd spread their cloaks on the road, and others cut branches from the trees and spread them on the road. And the crowds that went before him and that followed him were shouting, "Hosanna to the Son of David! Blessed is he who comes in the name of the Lord! Hosanna in the highest!"

Overall, Jesus was very reticent about making claims to be the Messiah. This was probably because he knew the claim would be misinterpreted, even by his own disciples. However, when the time of his passion approached, he made the boldest messianic claim he could make. He rode into Jerusalem at the time of the Passover in the profile of a king. Matthew certainly presents it that way with his quotation of Zechariah 9.9. Luke's account has the multitude shouting, "Blessed is the King who comes in the name of the Lord! Peace in heaven and glory in the highest!" So, Jesus came to Jerusalem as a king, as the Messiah in fact, but humbly, emphasizing the importance of humility in his kingdom.

Closely tied to humility is repentance, which both John the Baptizer and Jesus connected to the kingdom: "Repent, for the kingdom of heaven is at hand." During the last week of Jesus ministry he encountered opposition from various parties, including the scribes, Pharisees, and Sadducees. In response to their challenges, Jesus told several parables. The first of these was in Mt 21.28-32, which involved a following question to the hearers. Jesus said:

> What do you think? A man had two sons. And he went to the first and said, "Son, go and work in the vineyard today." And he answered, "I will not," but afterward he changed his mind and went. And he went to the other son and said the same. And he answered, "I go, sir," but did not go. Which of the two did the will of his father? They said, "The first." Jesus said to them, "Truly, I say to you, the tax collectors and the prostitutes go into the kingdom of God before you. For John came to you

> in the way of righteousness, and you did not believe him,
> but the tax collectors and the prostitutes believed him.
> And even when you saw it, you did not afterward change
> your minds and believe him."

Jesus said that the first son was like the Pharisees (cf. Matthew 21.45); they claimed to be doing God's will but then did not do it. The second son was like the well known sinners of Jesus' day, the harlots and the tax collectors. By their lives they had made it clear that they had no intention of serving God, but upon hearing Jesus' gospel, many of them repented of their wicked lifestyle and sought the kingdom. Jesus' point was that repentance was an essential characteristic in the kingdom and the door of the kingdom is open to whomever is willing to repent.

Love and Servanthood

We're outlining the basic principles of the kingdom of God. So far, there has been an emphasis on attitudes, especially submissiveness, humility and repentance. But there are more. This next episode is also during the last week of Jesus' life in the flesh and is taken from Mark 12.28-34 (cf. Mt 22.34-40):

> And one of the scribes came up and heard them
> disputing with one another, and seeing that he answered
> them well, asked him, "Which commandment is the most
> important of all?" Jesus answered, "The most important
> is, 'Hear, O Israel: The Lord our God, the Lord is one.
> And you shall love the Lord your God with all your heart
> and with all your soul and with all your mind and with all
> your strength.' The second is this: 'You shall love your
> neighbor as yourself.' There is no other commandment
> greater than these." And the scribe said to him, "You
> are right, Teacher. You have truly said that he is one, and
> there is no other besides him. And to love him with all
> the heart and with all the understanding and with all the
> strength, and to love one's neighbor as oneself, is much
> more than all whole burnt offerings and sacrifices." And
> when Jesus saw that he answered wisely, he said to him,
> "You are not far from the kingdom of God."

These two commandments are really one; to love one's neighbor as one-self *is* to love God with one's whole heart. And Jesus' final remark to the questioner shows how loving one's neighbor, and thereby loving God, is basic to the kingdom.

Love is closely tied to servanthood, a subject which Jesus tried to get across to his disciples in the episode of the rich young man. The last will be first, and the first last.

Baptism and the Lord's Supper

One of the few exchanges in the Gospel of John with regard to the kingdom took place in the days when Jesus was in the wilderness baptizing near John. This is Jesus' exchange with a Jewish ruler named Nicodemus (John 3.1-15). As is well known, the latter came to Jesus se-cretly, at night. It appears that he was very much impressed with Jesus. It's impossible to know how the conversation started, but at some point Jesus launched a new discussion with Nicodemus by asserting that:

"unless one is born again he cannot see the king-dom of God." Nicodemus said to him, "How can a man be born when he is old? Can he enter a second time into his mother's womb and be born?" Jesus answered, "Tru-ly, truly, I say to you, unless one is born of water and the Spirit, he cannot enter the kingdom of God. That which is born of the flesh is flesh, and that which is born of the Spirit is spirit. Do not marvel that I said to you, 'You must be born again.' The wind blows where it wishes, and you hear its sound, but you do not know where it comes from or where it goes. So it is with everyone who is born of the Spirit" (vv. 3-8).

From the context, it appears that the new birth, the one of water and the spirit, is baptism. In 3.22-24, Jesus and his disciples are found baptizing in the same area where John started baptizing, and this continued indefi-nitely (we think a good case can be made for Jesus continuing to baptize throughout his whole ministry). In 4.1-3 Jesus started accumulating even more disciples than John had, and this he did through baptizing them. So, it appears that for Jesus and John, being baptized in water was a rebirth, a spiritual rebirth, based on repentance, by which people were preparing themselves for entrance into the kingdom of God. This baptism which Jesus performed was a spiritual rebirth as opposed to a physical birth. It was a heavenly thing as opposed to an earthly thing (3.12).

Our next kingdom passage is taken from Mt 26.26-29 (cf. Mark 14.22-25 and Luke 22.15-20):

> Now as they were eating, Jesus took bread, and after blessing it broke it and gave it to the disciples, and said, "Take, eat; this is my body." And he took a cup, and when he had given thanks he gave it to them, saying, "Drink of it, all of you, for this is my blood of the covenant, which is poured out for many for the forgiveness of sins. I tell you I will not drink again of this fruit of the vine until that day when I drink it new with you in my Father's kingdom."

At Jesus' last Passover he instituted the Lord's Supper, a ritual which Jesus' followers continue to practice even today. This new Passover represented the new covenant which Jesus had established through his death on the cross. When disciples today participate in the Lord's Supper, they are eating the Passover with the Messiah in his spiritual kingdom. Where the old Passover was a celebration of Israel's redemption from Egyptian slavery, the new Passover is a celebration of redemption from sin for all those who are citizens of Jesus' kingdom.

Conclusion

This brings us to the end of the account of Jesus' ministry as found in the gospels, and here is what we can conclude at this point. Jesus came into the world to set up a spiritual kingdom; and since it is spiritual, it survives for all time. This was Jesus' mission. The headquarters for the kingdom are in heaven. This kingdom is the culmination of everything God had begun with Abraham, Moses, and the people of Israel. This kingdom is universal, comprised of people from all races and localities. This kingdom has to do primarily with how people think, or with states of heart, such as purity, peacefulness, penitence, servanthood and humility. The pinnacle of attitudes turns out to be loving God with one's whole heart, which is manifested in loving one's neighbor.

So, the kingdom of Christ is about attitudes, and for the citizen in Jesus' kingdom these matters must come before everything else in life. There are some rituals, though. Jesus connected the observance of the Lord's Supper and baptism with citizenship in the kingdom. So, these also are part of the eternal and spiritual kingdom of God. More will be said about these things in the summary chapters, but at this point we turn to other writings in the New Testament.

5 After Jesus' Resurrection

In the last two chapters we saw how central the concept of the kingdom of God was to Jesus' ministry as presented in the gospels, especially the Book of Matthew. Though those documents were written after Jesus was raised, they tell the story of his ministry. In this chapter we take up the documents in the rest of the New Testament. These will tell us how the kingdom of God was represented by the Twelve and the rest of Jesus' followers. Again, we shall present this data topically. We aim to show that Jesus did indeed succeed in transferring the mission of the kingdom to his followers. We'll see how the kingdom remained the central concept of the gospel, how the apostles saw the nature of the kingdom as spiritual, universal and eternal, and we'll see how they, under the inspiration of the Holy Spirit, were able to spell out clearly to both Jews and Gentiles what the demands of the kingdom were. The reader will notice a great deal of parallel with the gospel accounts, but that's as it should be.

The Kingdom as the Aim of Jesus' Mission

One of the best ways we can perceive the aims of Jesus is to see how those aims were perpetuated by his disciples. This takes us, first of all, to the Book of Acts. In Acts 1.1-12, Luke wrote:

> In the first book, O Theophilus, I have dealt with all that Jesus began to do and teach, until the day when he was taken up, after he had given commands through the Holy Spirit to the apostles whom he had chosen. He presented himself alive to them after his suffering by many proofs, appearing to them during forty days and speaking about the kingdom of God. And while staying with them he ordered them not to depart from Jerusalem, but to wait for the promise of the Father, which, he said, "you heard from me; for John baptized with water, but you will be baptized with the Holy Spirit not many days from now." So when they had come together, they asked him, "Lord, will you at this time restore the kingdom to Israel?" He said to them, "It is not for you to know times or seasons that the Father has fixed by his own authority. But you will receive power when the Holy Spirit has come upon you, and you will be my witnesses in Jerusalem and in all Judea and Samaria, and to the end of the earth." And when he had said these things, as they were looking on, he was lifted up, and a cloud took him out of their sight. And while they were gazing into heaven as he went, behold, two men stood by them in white robes, and said, "Men of Galilee, why do you stand looking into heaven? This Jesus, who was taken up from you into heaven, will come in the same way as you saw him go into heaven."

Luke makes the point that the main thesis of Jesus' post-resurrection instruction to his disciples was the kingdom of God. Now, in the rest of the Book of Acts one of the main themes in the various sermons we find there is that Jesus is the Christ, that is, the Messiah. But these terms mean king (we shall treat this matter later). The apostles presented Jesus as the anointed king over God's reestablished kingdom. However, for the rest of this chapter, we will look only at those passages that explicitly deal with the kingdom.

One can see from the story of apostolic preaching how the disciples continued the ministry of Jesus by proclaiming the kingdom, even though such a proclamation was an affront to the Roman emperor. In Thessalonica, Paul's opposition used this against him (Acts 17.5-8):

> But the Jews were jealous, and taking some wicked men of the rabble, they formed a mob, set the city in an uproar, and attacked the house of Jason, seeking to bring them out to the crowd. And when they could not find them, they dragged Jason and some of the brothers before the city authorities, shouting, "These men who have turned the world upside down have come here also, and Jason has received them, and they are all acting against the decrees of Caesar, saying that there is another king, Jesus." And the people and the city authorities were disturbed when they heard these things.

In fact, it appears that the phrase "the kingdom of God" was for Luke a term that referred to gospel preaching. The kingdom was the subject of Philip's message to the Samaritans (Acts 8.4-25). In Acts 19.8-10, it says that Paul spent his time arguing and pleading about the kingdom of God for many months in Corinth. In 20.25, Paul referred to his preaching as "preaching the kingdom". And finally in Acts 28, when a party of Jews in Rome came to see Paul, it is said that Paul spent his time testifying to them about the kingdom of God (vv.23, 31). So, in the Book of Acts, the basic gospel was referred to as a message about the impending fulfillment of God's plan for the world by the coming of the Christ's kingdom, and when people came to believe in that message, as we shall see, they were baptized in the name of Jesus the Christ (Messiah) in order to enter that kingdom.

This emphasis on the kingdom is found in the epistles, too. In Colossians 4.10-17, Paul mentions his "fellow workers for the kingdom of God". Paul saw those people who worked side by side with him as people who were giving their lives, promoting the eternal, spiritual kingdom of God. In a similar vein, Paul encouraged the young man Timothy to be urgent about preaching the word. The basis of this urgency was the kingdom of Christ (2 Timothy 4.1-5). Paul saw faithfulness to the word of the gospel as essential to the kingdom. Though he does not set out the contents of that preaching in this passage, he does make it clear that citizenship in Christ's kingdom does require faithfulness to the word of God, which has come into the world through Christ and his apostles.

Finally, we come to the Book of Revelation, which is shot through with kingdom talk. It opens as follows (1.4-9):

> John to the seven churches that are in Asia: Grace to you and peace from him who is and who was and who is to come, and from the seven spirits who are before his throne, and from Jesus Christ the faithful witness, the firstborn of the dead, and the ruler of kings on earth.
>
> To him who loves us and has freed us from our sins by his blood and made us a kingdom, priests to his God and Father, to him be glory and dominion forever and ever. Amen. Behold, he is coming with the clouds, and every eye will see him, even those who p i e r c e d him, and all tribes of the earth will wail on account of him. Even so. Amen.
>
> "I am the Alpha and the Omega," says the Lord God, "who is and who was and who is to come, the Almighty."
>
> I, John, your brother and partner in the tribulation and the kingdom and the patient endurance that are in Jesus, was on the island called Patmos on account of the word of God and the testimony of Jesus.

In the opening vision, God is seated on his throne, with Christ standing beside him, occupying the position of ruler of Kings. The writer then makes the point that followers of Christ comprise a kingdom, a kingdom of priests (very much like 1 Peter 2.4.ff.). Then the statement is made that God's dominion is forever and ever. And finally, in vs. 9, John, the writer, addresses his audience as those who share citizenship in the kingdom. This is definitely a picture of the kingdom of God with Christians as citizens in that kingdom. The parallels between Christianity and the Israelites is quite manifest. The language here is drawn from Exodus 19.4-6, where God told the Israelites under Moses' leadership that he was making out of them a kingdom of priests. This depiction of Christians as the kingdom of God continues throughout, culminating with the victory of God (cf. 19.6).

The rest of the Book of Revelation carries out this kingdom

theme even further. It is our interpretation that the historical context of this book is about the fall of Jerusalem and the fall of Rome, which were imminent (seventh decade of the first century). So, just as Yahweh defeated the Egyptians in the days of Moses, the Christians, under the leadership of Jesus, would defeat Rome. Later, in fact, the writer pictures the triumphant people of God standing on the shore, like the shore of the Red Sea in Exodus, and singing the song of Moses, only this time it can also be called the Song of the Lamb (Revelation 15. 2-4).

The Spiritual Nature of the Kingdom

In a passage we shall look at more closely below, 1 Corinthians 15, Paul closes out his discussion of resurrection with the following remark, "I tell you this, brothers: flesh and blood cannot inherit the kingdom of God, nor does the perishable inherit the imperishable" (vs. 50). We will take up again the question of the timing of the kingdom, but what is essential here is that a follower of Christ needs to be engaged in kingdom living, whether he believes that the kingdom has already come, or that it is to come in the future, or even that both are true in some sense. Paul's remark at this point is profoundly important: the kingdom of God is spirituality in contrast to physicality, so what is imperishable should come before the perishable. We are reminded of Romans 14.17, where Paul said, similarly, that the kingdom of God is not about food but rather about righteousness, peace, and joy. These things are not perishable; these things are spiritual. In our efforts to extract from the scriptures the eternal principles of Christianity, we find the essential characteristic of spirituality. It actually stands to reason that what would abide century after century, culture to culture for all time, is what is spiritual and imperishable, not what is tied to the flesh. Dieters sometimes have to deal with the issue of, not only what not to eat, but also what kinds of things should be eaten. It's not enough to stop eating the wrong foods; the healthy dieter must learn to eat good things. In the same way, the kingdom of God is not just about stopping certain behaviors, but learning to replace the physical with the spiritual. Paul's words to Timothy are relevant here (1 Timothy 6.13-16):

I charge you in the presence of God, who gives life to all things, and of Christ Jesus, who in his testimony before Pontius Pilate made the good confession, to keep the commandment unstained and free from reproach until the appearing of our Lord Jesus C h r i s t , which he will display at the proper time—he who is the blessed and only Sovereign, the King of kings and Lord of lords, who alone has immortality, who dwells in unapproachable light, whom no one has ever seen or can see. To him be honor and eternal dominion. Amen.

Jesus is the Unseen King of an Unseen Kingdom.

In a sermon we call the Book of Hebrews the preacher makes a sustained argument for the superiority of Christianity over Judaism in an effort to keep Jewish Christians from abandoning the new faith and returning to their roots. The writer ends his sermon by comparing the kingdom of Christ to the old kingdom of Israel, which was established at Mt. Sinai (12.18-29). His point is that disciples of Christ have come to a better mountain:

> For you have not come to what may be touched, a blazing fire and darkness and gloom and a tempest and the sound of a trumpet and a voice whose words made the hearers beg that no further messages be spoken to them. For they could not endure the order that was given, "If even a beast touches the mountain, it shall be stoned." Indeed, so terrifying was the sight that Moses said, "I tremble with fear." But you have come to M o u n t Zion and to the city of the living God, the heavenly Jerusalem, and to innumerable angels in festal gathering, and to the assembly of the firstborn who are enrolled in heaven, and to God, the judge of all, and to the spirits of the righteous made perfect, and to Jesus, the mediator of a new covenant, and to the sprinkled blood that speaks a better word than the blood of Abel.
>
> See that you do not refuse him who is speaking. For if they did not escape when they refused him who warned them on earth, much less will we escape if we reject him who warns from heaven. At that time his

voice shook the earth, but now he has promised, "Yet once more I will shake not only the earth but also the heavens." This phrase, "Yet once more," indicates the removal of things that are shaken—that is, things that have been made—in order that the things that cannot be shaken may remain. Therefore let us be grateful for receiving a kingdom that cannot be shaken, and thus let us offer to God acceptable worship, with reverence and awe, for our God is a consuming fire.

The language of spirituality, as opposed to physicality, could not be stronger. Christianity is better because it is spiritual. Not only does he call it the heavenly Jerusalem but also a kingdom, a kingdom which can never be shaken.

Revelation 5.8-10 pictures the throne room of God in heaven. Twenty-four elders surround God's throne, and they sing "a new song", which refers to Jesus' death on the cross for all people of every nation, and God's having "made them a kingdom and priests to our God", and how they "shall reign on the earth." There is no physical sense in which Christians in the apostolic age reigned on earth. God would win a victory over their persecutors, it is true, but their reign was an unseen reign (cf. 20.4-6).

In Revelation 16.10-14, we have another picture of God's victory over evil, represented as a ferocious beast. But as the result of the work of Christ, the beast's kingdom is thrown into darkness, and its citizens are punished. God's kingdom is a spiritual kingdom; its concerns are with spiritual and eternal matters. Its king, the Messiah, does not rule over an earthly institution but rules in the hearts of righteous men. But having said that, chapter 17 points out that the evil kingdom, mentioned above, can be manifested in many physical forms. We believe that chapter 17 is a picture of the Roman Empire; the harlot sitting on the beast is Rome. Rome had dominion over all the kings of the earth (vs. 18), and Rome persecuted Jesus followers (vs. 6). The story swells to vs. 14, where the evil henchmen of Satan make war on the Lamb, but "the Lamb will conquer them, for he is Lord of lords and King of kings, and those with him will be called chosen and faithful".

The Kingdom is Eternal

Such is surely suggested by Paul's statement to Timothy (1Timothy 1.15-17):

> The saying is trustworthy and deserving of full acceptance, that Christ Jesus came into the world to save sinners, of whom I am the foremost. But I received mercy for this reason, that in me, as the foremost, Jesus Christ might display his perfect patience as an example to those who were to believe in him for eternal life. To the King of the ages, immortal, invisible, the only God, be honor and glory forever and ever. Amen.

As we saw above with regard to Hebrews 12.18-29, the new kingdom of God, which Christ brought into the world, can never be shaken. In Hebrews 1.8-10, the writer, or we should say, the preacher, uses passages from the Psalms to extol Jesus' place in God's kingdom. The main point of these verses is that Jesus' kingdom is eternal.

> But of the Son he says,
> "Your throne, O God, is forever and ever,
> the scepter of uprightness is the scepter of your kingdom."

Verse 8 is very important to our thesis, namely, that what is eternally obligatory about the New Testament is the kingdom of Christ. If Jesus came to set up the eternal, spiritual kingdom of God, then those aspects of the kingdom which we find in the New Testament are incumbent upon all Christians in all places for all times. That means that not every word in the New Testament is directly applicable, and clearly not incumbent, upon all disciples for all times, but only those aspects of Jesus' kingdom which we find in those texts.

The seventh trumpet of the Book of Revelation (11.15-18) continues the theme of the Book of Revelation that there is an eternal, spiritual kingdom of God on earth and that it transcends all other authorities and powers. The Book of Revelation is indeed extraordinary for impressing on the reader the true greatness of God's kingdom:

> Then the seventh angel blew his trumpet, and there were loud voices in heaven, saying, "The kingdom of the world has become the kingdom of our Lord and of his Christ, and he shall reign forever and ever." And the twenty-four elders who sit on their thrones before God

fell on their faces and worshiped God, saying:

"We give thanks to you, Lord God Almighty,
who is and who was,
for you have taken your great power
and begun to reign.
The nations raged,
but your wrath came,
and the time for the dead to be judged,
and for rewarding your servants,
          the prophets and saints,
and those who fear your name,
both small and great,
and for destroying the destroyers of the earth."

Finally, in the vision of the heavenly Jerusalem (Revelation 22.3-5) we find something similar:

No longer will there be anything accursed, but the throne of God and of the Lamb will be in it, and his servants will worship him. They will see his face, and his name will be on their foreheads. And night will be no more. They will need no light of lamp or sun, for the Lord God will be their light, and they will reign forever and ever.

The Kingdom is Universal

It is manifestly obvious, once the reader gets outside the gospels, how the gospel of the kingdom of Christ was intended for all ethnic groups. The first major tension in the church, according to the Book of Acts, was over the inclusion of Gentiles. This can also clearly be seen in Revelation 5.8-10,

And when he had taken the scroll, the four living creatures and the twenty-four elders fell down before the Lamb, each holding a harp, and golden bowls full of incense, which are the prayers of the saints. And they sang a new song, saying:

"Worthy are you to take the scroll
          and to open its seals,
for you were slain, and by your blood you

> ransomed people for God
> from every tribe and language and people
> and nation,
> and you have made them a kingdom and
> priests to our God,
> and they shall reign on the earth."

See also Revelation 15.3-4.

The Imminence of the Kingdom

The apostles and early leaders in the Jesus movement saw themselves as working to bring about the entrance of the kingdom of God to earth. This issue is a large area of concern in New Testament study, but we saw in Chapter 3 of this book how Jesus promised the coming of the kingdom to occur in the lifetimes of his followers. We see this in statements like Paul's (2 Timothy 4.18), "The Lord will rescue me from every evil deed and bring me safely into his heavenly kingdom."

But the best place to start is 1 Corinthians 15.20-28:

> But in fact Christ has been raised from the dead, the firstfruits of those who have fallen asleep. For as by a man came death, by a man has come also the resurrection of the dead. For as in Adam all die, so also in Christ shall all be made alive. But each in his own order: Christ the firstfruits, then at his coming those who belong to Christ. Then comes the end, when he delivers the kingdom to God the Father after destroying every rule and every authority and power. For he must reign until he has put all his enemies under his feet. The last enemy to be destroyed is death. For "God has put all things in subjection under his feet." But when it says, "all things are put in subjection," it is plain that he is excepted who put all things in subjection under him. When all things are subjected to him, then the Son himself will also be subjected to him who put all things in subjection under him, that God may be all in all.

This paragraph comes in the middle of a lengthy discussion about the resurrection of Jesus and its implications for the resurrection of believers. Paul makes the statement that Christ, in a very special sense, was the first to be raised from the dead and then at his coming there would occur the resurrection of those who belong to Christ. Between these two moments Jesus was to reign and destroy all his enemies, the last of which would be death. At this point, the end of the age would occur "when he delivers the kingdom to God the Father after destroying every rule and every authority and every power." We are aware that there are more than a few interpretations of the second coming of Christ, the end of the world, the resurrection of the dead and the meaning of this paragraph. But first of all, let this be said. It does not really matter for our purposes in this book which interpretation is actually true; we can all agree that as Christians we need to be engaged in kingdom living. So, whether one believes the kingdom has already been established, or that it is to be established at some later time, or whether both are true in one sense or the other, disciples of Christ should always be engaged in kingdom living. A major point of this paragraph, though, is that the main purpose of Jesus' coming into this world was to establish the kingdom of God. We, the authors, in fact, lean toward a preterist interpretation, by which the end of the age came in connection with the destruction of Jerusalem in the first century. We believe this especially coheres with the idea of a spiritual kingdom. However, the main concern of our book is to set out what is essential to Christian living for all Christians for all times, and we would argue that one's particular interpretation of the end times is not one of those essentials but that the nature of kingdom living is.

In our day and time, there is much discussion, sometimes even vitriol, over the second coming of Christ and the end of the age. We would suggest that sometimes citizens of Christ's kingdom violate essential, eternal principals of kingdom living, while debating with their fellow citizens the doctrine of the second coming of Christ, which itself is not a kingdom essential. We can all agree that there is a kingdom of God. Paul told his audience to be seriously engaged in kingdom living with a view toward the coming of the kingdom. As we just said, we have our own interpretation of the timing of Jesus' coming and of the end of the age, but that itself is not a kingdom issue. Kingdom living is. We are reminded of an incident in our own lives which illustrates this very point. On a certain occasion, a church that we know of became embroiled in a hot debate over the currency of spiritual gifts, such as tongue speaking and prophecy. A meeting was called to discuss, or perhaps even to settle, this argument. An octogenarian was at the meeting and asked to start the meeting with a reading of 1 Corinthians 13, wherein Paul asserts that love is more important that any of these spiritual gifts and that it is more important to encourage and build up the body than to exercise the gift of prophesy or the gift of tongues. However, the old man was immediately shut down with the statement that "This meeting has been called to discuss the meat of the word." This is our point. Sometimes Christians invert the issues of Christianity, placing far lesser matters above essential principals of the kingdom. As we have seen, love is one of those essential principles of the kingdom; spiritual gifts are not. Our concern in this book is to elucidate what is central to the kingdom, what is incumbent upon all Christians for all times in every place.

Having said that, though, we close on the imminence of the kingdom with the vision in Revelation 12.7-12, in which a war breaks out in heaven between angels and demons. Satan gets thrown down to earth, resulting in his defeat, which means that all of his accusations against God's people are rendered null and void. It can be said, at that point in the Book of Revelation, that the power and the kingdom of God had finally come. The kingdom of God is about the defeat of evil, and that defeat was procured in the work of Christ. One is reminded again of Exodus 15, where Moses exulted over the defeat of Pharaoh and sang about the kingdom of God.

The Demands of the Kingdom

We want to determine what exactly is required of all citizens of God's kingdom, no matter what time, what race, what culture or what place. Certain things were essential to entrance into the kingdom. One would expect faith in God, Christ and the gospel to be among them. And so we find Paul saying to the disciples in Thessalonica that the dividing line between those who would exist in the presence of the Lord in the kingdom and those who would not was belief in his testimony to them, that is, those who believed in the gospel were in the kingdom, and therefore belief in the gospel was a trait essential to the kingdom (cf. 1

Thessalonians 2.13).

The writers of the New Testament also insisted on an attitude of submission to the royal authority of Jesus. Earlier in this chapter we cited Hebrews 12, where he pictured the Christians of his day as about to receive a new kingdom, a spiritual one which could never be shaken. Therefore, they should not refuse Christ. He then compared their situation to the Israelites at Mt. Sinai. If those of the former kingdom who refused Moses did not escape punishment, much less would they escape if they rejected him who warned them "from heaven" (vv.25-29).

Another example can be found in 1 Corinthians 4. As is well known, this is part of a discussion about disciples lining up behind human teachers. Apparently, some of the members of the church in Corinth had exalted themselves to positions of power in the church and were creating dissension. Paul contrasted himself with these teachers as a paterfamilias, the father of a large family, might be contrasted with hired teachers or tutors (4.15). Since some of these tutors had created a lot of dissension in Corinth, Paul says that he had sent Timothy to them to remind them of his ways in Christ. However, Paul went on to say:

> Some are arrogant, as though I were not coming
> to you. But I will come to you soon, if the Lord wills,
> and I will find out not the talk of these arrogant people
> but their power. For the kingdom of God does not con-
> sist in talk but in power. What do you wish? Shall I come
> to you with a rod, or with love in a spirit of gentleness?

One is reminded of the close of the Sermon on the Mount, where the people were astonished at Jesus' teachings, because he taught them as one who had divine authority and not as one of the scribes of his day (Matthew 7.28-29). Jesus clearly presented himself to the people of his day as an authoritative spokesman of God. Accordingly, Paul was on his way to Corinth, and he would manifest himself as a divine spokesman, much superior to those quarrelsome would-be teachers there. The Corinthian church was like a classroom of disorderly students with the teacher out of the room. So, Paul's picture of the kingdom of God clearly entailed the concept that it rested on God's own authority and was not just the culmination of mere human thinking. That also meant that those in the kingdom should be obedient to proper authorities.

Baptism also plays a role. For example, in Acts 8.12 we read about Philip coming to Samaria:

> But when they believed Philip as he preached
> good news about the kingdom of God and the name of
> Jesus Christ, they were baptized, both men and women.
> Even Simon himself believed, and after being baptized
> he continued with Philip. And seeing signs and great
> miracles performed, he was amazed.

John and Jesus were both baptizers, and Jesus had stipulated baptism as the proper response to the kingdom message.

Baptism, as we have seen, puts one in the kingdom, but the new citizen should feel both an appreciation for this as well as a sense of responsibility. In 1Thessalonians 2.9-12 we find Paul saying to the Thessalonian converts:

> For you remember, brothers, our labor and toil:
> we worked night and day, that we might not be a burden
> to any of you, while we proclaimed to you the gospel
> of God. You are witnesses, and God also, how holy and
> righteous and blameless was our conduct toward you be-
> lievers. For you know how, like a father with his chil-
> dren, we exhorted each one of you and encouraged you
> and charged you to walk in a manner worthy of God,
> who calls you into his own kingdom and glory.

There is a "walk", a lifestyle, that is worthy of the kingdom. The purpose of the gospel is to call people into that kingdom lifestyle (cf. 2 Thessalonians 2.14).

The Book of 1 Peter was dedicated to the problem of how to live a life in service to Christ in the midst of a hostile cultural environment. Peter warned the disciples they would need to get their minds around the difficulty of living a holy life in the middle of all the pressures of the Roman Empire. In a central statement that we find in 2.4-10, Peter referred to the disciples as a spiritual temple made out of living stones with Jesus as the cornerstone:

> As you come to him, a living stone rejected by
> men but in the sight of God chosen and precious, you
> yourselves like living stones are being built up as a
> spiritual house, to be a holy priesthood, to offer spiritual
> sacrifices acceptable to God through Jesus Christ. For it

stands in Scripture:

> "Behold, I am laying in Zion a stone,
> a cornerstone chosen and precious,
> and whoever believes in him will not be
> put to shame."

So the honor is for you who believe, but for those who do not believe:

> "The stone that the builders rejected
> has become the cornerstone,"

and

> "A stone of stumbling,
> and a rock of offense."

They stumble because they disobey the word, as they were destined to do.

But you are a chosen race, a royal priesthood, a holy nation, a people for his own possession, that you may proclaim the excellencies of him who called you out of darkness into his marvelous light. Once you were not a people, but now you are God's people; once you had not received mercy, but now you have received mercy.

Many unbelievers, Peter said, would stumble over that stone, but believers had not only accepted Jesus as the cornerstone, but in the words of Exodus 19, they had also been made into a royal priesthood and a holy nation. Just as the people of Israel in the Old Testament were supposed to reflect the glory of God to the Gentile world, the Christians, as God's new "chosen race", were to "declare the wonderful deeds of him who called you out of darkness into his marvelous light". The rest of the Book of 1 Peter was a handbook for these early Christians to show them how to reflect the light of God to the Roman world. The term 'royal priesthood', borrowed from Exodus 19, is a kingdom term. The people of Israel were not just another kingdom, but God's kingdom, where on some level it could be said that every citizen of that kingdom was a priest. Similarly, the new kingdom of Christ is a kingdom of holiness. This kingdom passage sets out two major aspects of kingdom living, holiness and evangelism. So, let's see what the apostles and leaders of the early church said about holy living.

In Romans 14-15, Paul engaged the disciples with regard to issues such as diet and holy days. His point was that what one eats and what days one observes are irrelevant to his service to God. In 14.17-18, he says "For the kingdom of God is not a matter of eating and drinking but of righteousness and peace and joy in the Holy Spirit. Whoever thus serves Christ is acceptable to God and approved by men." In this, Paul sounds a lot like Jesus. The kingdom of God is focused on godly attitudes rather than on physical rituals. Righteousness in the Book of Romans has to do with being right before God. Peace, as in vs. 19, means getting along with one another. Joy, as in the Book of Philippians, has to do with cheerfulness. These are godly states and attitudes, and that, for Paul, is what the kingdom was about.

The apostles and leaders of the early church took the gospel of the kingdom to a wide range of communities. In what follows we shall show, in rather rapid succession, what they told their followers was necessary to their heavenly citizenship.

We start with 1 Corinthians (vv. 6.9-11):

> Or do you not know that the unrighteous will not inherit the kingdom of God? Do not be deceived: neither the sexually immoral, nor idolaters, nor adulterers, nor men who practice homosexuality, nor thieves, nor the greedy, nor drunkards, nor revilers, nor swindlers will inherit the kingdom of God. And such were some of you. But you were washed, you were sanctified, you were justified in the name of the Lord Jesus Christ and by the Spirit of our God.

This would have to be one of the clearer passages about kingdom living. Paul was preparing these early believers for their entrance into the kingdom of God, the arrival of which was imminent. Because of that, the disciples needed to be engaged in kingdom living. All of the things he mentions here, which include idolatry, homosexual behavior, greed and drunkenness, would keep someone out of the kingdom. Here are some characteristics which would have to be true of all citizens of God's kingdom for all time, including our day and the future.

In the verses that follow (12-20), Paul expanded on these kingdom principals with the basic point that a citizen of the kingdom was not to be enslaved by any sort of fleshly passion. He ends up the following paragraph with these words: "You are not your own; you were bought with a price. So glorify God in your body." An eternal principal for Christians is that they will not be enslaved by their bodily passions, but will use their physical bodies to bring glory to God.

Leaving 1 Corinthians, we come to Galatians 5.16-24. This passage is directly relevant to our concerns. The churches of Galatia had become embroiled in a controversy over the Law of Moses. Some of Paul's enemies had followed him into the various churches he had established and had prevailed upon the new converts to accept the Law of Moses, along with circumcision and other Jewish practices, as essential to their salvation in Christ. This deals with our question exactly: what is indeed essential to the kingdom? In the passage cited above, Paul says, very much like 1 Corinthians 15.50, that it is the spiritual that is essential to the kingdom, and the flesh thwarts one's entrance into the kingdom:

> But I say, walk by the Spirit, and you will not gratify the desires of the flesh. For the desires of the flesh are against the Spirit, and the desires of the Spirit are against the flesh, for these are opposed to each other, to keep you from doing the things you want to do. But if you are led by the Spirit, you are not under the law. Now the works of the flesh are evident: sexual immorality, impurity, sensuality, idolatry, sorcery, enmity, strife, jealousy, fits of anger, rivalries, dissensions, divisions, envy, drunkenness, orgies, and things like these. I warn you, as I warned you before, that those who do such things will not inherit the kingdom of God. But the fruit of the Spirit is love, joy, peace, patience, kindness, goodness, faithfulness, gentleness, self-control; against such things there is no law. And those who belong to Christ Jesus have crucified the flesh with its passions and desires.

Paul pits spirit against flesh. (Your authors think the reference here is to spirit, as opposed to flesh, and not the Holy Spirit.) It seems clear that whether or not the Galatians followed the teaching of the Old Testament was irrelevant; what is not irrelevant is kingdom living. If one is spiritually minded, he will eschew certain fleshly activities, and in their place pursue the fruit of the spirit. As with end times, there are many views in Christendom on the role of the Holy Spirit. Once again, it's less important which one of these views, if any, is accepted than whether one eschews the flesh and follows spirit. In this passage, which is very much like 1 Corinthians 6.9-11, Paul spelled out what is essential to the kingdom, namely the avoidance of the works of the flesh and the living out of the fruit of the spirit. Fleshly things are to be disciplined; the spiritual is to be pursued. This again brings emphasis to the point that the kingdom of Christ is a spiritual kingdom. It is all about spirituality, as opposed to that which is fleshly. There are many "flesh vs. spirit" passages in the New Testament; when we are reading those passages we are in fact reading about the kingdom of Christ.

When we come to Ephesians 5.3-5, we come again to a list of negative behaviors:

> But sexual immorality and all impurity or covet-
> ousness must not even be named among you, as is proper
> among saints. Let there be no filthiness nor foolish talk
> nor crude joking, which are out of place, but instead let
> there be thanksgiving. For you may be sure of this, that
> everyone who is sexually immoral or impure, or who is
> covetous (that is, an idolater), has no inheritance in the
> kingdom of Christ and God.

Paul says here again that those who engage in these activities do not have "any inheritance in the kingdom of Christ and of God." He goes on to use language about light and darkness, the point of which is that these lifestyle matters are critical to one's life in the kingdom. Once again, the works of the flesh are what keep a person out of the eternal, spiritual kingdom of Christ.

Traditionally, Paul's letters to the Ephesians and Colossians have been studied together, since the content of the two letters is so similar. One has only to rearrange some of the paragraphs of one of the letters to see that Paul is using the same themes to address the various problems in each of these churches. We want to keep that in mind as we turn to Colossians 1.13-20 (cf. Ephesians 1.19-23), "He has delivered us from the domain of darkness and transferred us to the kingdom of his beloved Son, in whom we have redemption, the forgiveness of sins." Several times in the New Testament we come across the appellation, "King of kings and Lord and lords" (1Timothy 6.15, Revelation 17.14,

19.16, 5.10). Paul here in Colossians uses some very interesting additional words, words like darkness and light (1.12). One could at this point go through the letters to the Ephesians and Colossians and look at references to kingdom and light and gain further insights into the nature of the kingdom.

2 Peter 1.3-11 is a truly extraordinary passage with regard to the kingdom of God. The writer was concerned about people falling away from the kingdom, so he set out the growth pattern of the individual disciple necessary to entering and staying in "the eternal kingdom of our Lord and Savior Jesus Christ.":

> His divine power has granted to us all things that pertain to life and godliness, through the knowledge of him who called us to his own glory and excellence, by which he has granted to us his precious and very great promises, so that through them you may become partakers of the divine nature, having escaped from the corruption that is in the world because of sinful desire. For this very reason, make every effort to supplement your faith with virtue, and virtue with knowledge, and knowledge with self-control, and self-control with steadfastness, and steadfastness with godliness, and godliness with brotherly affection, and brotherly affection with love. For if these qualities are yours and are increasing, they keep you from being ineffective or unfruitful in the knowledge of our Lord Jesus Christ. For whoever lacks these qualities is so nearsighted that he is blind, having forgotten that he was cleansed from his former sins. Therefore, brothers, be all the more diligent to confirm your calling and election, for if you practice these qualities you will never fall. For in this way there will be richly provided for you an entrance into the eternal kingdom of our Lord and Savior Jesus Christ.

Once again, we find that the kingdom is primarily about principles, and we're blessed even today to have such a clear list of principles that are stated to be essential to kingdom living. There couldn't be a clearer passage.

Another thing that is often associated with the kingdom is the willingness, even the expectation, to suffer. Citizens of this new kingdom should expect trouble. For example, in Acts 14.21-22, Paul and Barnabas returned from Derbe, a city on their first missionary journey, and visited all of the churches they had already planted. "When they had preached the gospel to that city and had made many disciples, they returned to Lystra and to Iconium and to Antioch, strengthening the souls of the disciples, encouraging them to continue in the faith, and saying that through many tribulations we must enter the kingdom of God."

In Paul's second letter to the Thessalonian disciples, in 1.3-12, he wrote:

> We ought always to give thanks to God for you, brothers, as is right, because your faith is growing abundantly, and the love of every one of you for one another is increasing. Therefore we ourselves boast about you in the churches of God for your steadfastness and faith in all your persecutions and in the afflictions that you are enduring. This is evidence of the righteous judgment of God, that you may be considered worthy of the kingdom of God, for which you are also suffering— since indeed God considers it just to repay with affliction those who afflict you, and to grant relief to you who are afflicted as well as to us, when the Lord Jesus is revealed from heaven with his mighty angels in flaming fire, inflicting vengeance on those who do not know God and on those who do not obey the gospel of our Lord Jesus. They will suffer the punishment of eternal destruction, away from the presence of the Lord and from the glory of his might, when he comes on that day to be glorified in his saints, and to be marveled at among all who have believed, because our testimony to you was believed. To this end we always pray for you, that our God may make you worthy of his calling and may fulfill every resolve for good and every work of faith by his power, so that the name of our Lord Jesus may be glorified in you, and you in him, according to the grace of our God and the Lord Jesus Christ.

Paul extolled their willingness to suffer for the kingdom. He even made the point that these sufferings that they had endured, primarily as a result of persecution, had served to make them worthy of the kingdom of God. Paul went on to talk about the coming of the Lord Jesus in their future. As we said under 1 Corinthians 15, there are lots of different views on the second coming of Christ: premillennialism, post-millennialism, amillennialism, spiritual millennialism, and even preterism. Our point, though, is that none of these millennial views matters to The Kingdom Algorithm. All eschatological theorists hold that we should live according to kingdom principles, so one's eschatology is irrelevant on this point.

Another question that arises from this passage is whether suffering persecution is essential to the kingdom. It states in the passage that such sufferings had made the Thessalonian disciples worthy of the kingdom, and though that serves as an example to us, it does not follow from this passage that being persecuted is an essential quality of the kingdom. However, that said, wisdom behooves all followers of Christ to be prepared to pay whatever prices he might have to pay in order to live in the kingdom. History is replete with examples of citizens of God's kingdom who were persecuted because of their resoluteness to live the kingdom life. It does appear that from time to time that God has used suffering to sort out those who are in the kingdom from those who are not. John also, in Revelation 1.9, conjoins the notions of 'kingdom' and 'tribulation'. This is a theme that runs throughout the Book of Revelation. However, the Book of Revelation is more of a depiction of the glory of God's kingdom, the kingdom of Christ, than it is a detailed explanation of what that kingdom means. But certainly it is an encouraging picture because of the victory it describes.

Conclusion

In Chapters Three and Four above, we surveyed kingdom texts from the gospels. Chapter Five has surveyed the rest of the New Testament texts, which are a bit less monolithic. However, there is clearly a unified picture of the kingdom of Christ from these various writings. First of all, it is made clear that the express mission of Jesus was to set up the newest stage of the kingdom of God. The writers contrasted the physical aspects of the Old Testament kingdom with the spiritual aspects of Jesus' kingdom, emphasizing its superiority. In this new kingdom the ultimate truth about God's plan for human beings would be expressed. Not only did Jesus consciously inaugurate this new kingdom, but its imminent arrival was the main point of early gospel preaching. The Twelve and the early apostles were charged with authoritative roles in the Kingdom. Secondly, in the texts discussed in this chapter, there is also to be found a clear depiction of Jesus' kingdom. Because of the cross, Jesus has been made king of an eternal and spiritual kingdom. This kingdom trumps all earthly authority, and even the spiritual authority of Satan. It also secures eternal life for its citizens. Thirdly, God works to help people to enter this kingdom, as well as to stay in it, but there are also things people must do. Belief in the message of the gospel of the kingdom was necessary. Also, people enter the kingdom by being baptized into it, in the name of Jesus the Messiah, and some continuous effort on their part has to be exerted. They would have to withstand tribulation, should it come, which would require struggle on their part. There are behaviors which would exclude them from the kingdom, such as works of the flesh, as well as behaviors which were required by their citizenship, such as love, preeminently, and also righteousness, peace and joy, the fruits of the Spirit, the things from "above" and principles of spiritual growth.

This is a brief summary, but in a later chapter we will attempt a description of the universal citizen in the kingdom of Christ.

6 A Kingdom By Any Other Name

We are trying to set out and defend a simple algorithm for taking passages from the biblical texts and applying them directly to our lives. We want to take the nebulousness out of the matter. We have enunciated that algorithm several times, but basically it involves looking in the Bible for kingdom statements. However, just as we showed in our discussion of the confrontation between Jesus and the rich young ruler (Matthew 19.16-30, Mark 10.17-31, Luke 18.18-30), we are aware that there are phrases, words and pairs of words, other than the word "kingdom" which carry the idea of Jesus' kingdom. In that story itself there were the words such as, "treasure in heaven", "kingdom of heaven", "kingdom of God", "new world" and "throne", all of which were employed by Matthew as virtually interchangeable terms. Others we have come across include "lord/servant", "ruler/subject", "authority/submission", as well as "Messiah (Christ)", "anointed", "right hand of God", "firstborn", "power", "name", "dominion" and "crown". Consider, for example, Colossians 1.9-20, a passage to which we will turn several times in this chapter:

And so, from the day we heard, we have not ceased to pray for you, asking that you may be filled with the knowledge of his will in all spiritual wisdom and understanding, so as to walk in a manner worthy of the Lord, fully pleasing to him, bearing fruit in every good work and increasing in the knowledge of God. May you be strengthened with all power, according to his glorious might, for all endurance and patience with joy, giving thanks to the Father, who has qualified you to share in the inheritance of the saints in light. He has delivered us from the domain of darkness and transferred us to the kingdom of his beloved Son, in whom we have redemption, the forgiveness of sin.

He is the image of the invisible God, the firstborn of all creation. For by him all things were created, in heaven and on earth, visible and invisible, whether thrones or dominions or rulers or authorities — all things were created through him and for him. And he is before all things, and in him all things hold together. And he is the head of the body, the church. He is the beginning, the firstborn from the dead, that in everything he might be preeminent. For in him all the fullness of God was pleased to dwell, and through him to reconcile to himself all things, whether on earth or in heaven, making peace by the blood of his cross.

This passage clearly shows how other words are interchangeable with the word "kingdom".

So, we are very aware that the biblical writers could speak in certain passages of the kingdom without using the word "kingdom", therefore those other passages as well would be kingdom passages and be subject to the algorithm. But we need to be careful; we mustn't choose terms willy-nilly. The connections among these kingdom terms have to be established from the Bible itself. We have combed the New Testament for just those connections, and in this chapter we intend to show how "kingdom" is connected to "authority", for example, and additionally to show what implications "authority", as well as the other additional terms, have for the life of the modern day Bible reader. Now, whereas the kingdom of God is a metaphor based on the image of a glistening city ruled by God and His Christ, a metaphor which easily lends itself to setting out conditions for citizenship therein, these additional terms do not so lend themselves. However, they do call for some attention. So, we will want to survey these terms as well to see what beliefs, practices and characteristics might be added to our list of kingdom essentials. In other words, when we examine the essential nature of these named ideas, we want to see what new elements might be found. We also might add that the reader should expect the passages often to overlap passages which have already been addressed. In such cases, our treatment of those passages in the following paragraphs will be brief.

Christ

First of all, the word "Christ" is the anglicized Greek word for the anglicized Hebrew word "Messiah" (cf. John 1.41), which means anointed one. Christ, then, is a title, and as such it means king, since in the relevant contexts Jesus is the anointed king. (It is also connected to Sonship, Matthew 16.16 and Lord, Acts 3.36.) However, in most of the passages, the terms are used as just that, titles; Jesus Christ is the nomenclature for the resurrected Jesus. In many passages, especially in Acts, the point is to prove that in fact Jesus is the Messiah. So, despite the great importance of these passages in other contexts, they do not add much to our understanding of the nature of the kingdom or what is required to enter and stay in that kingdom, except once again to emphasize how indeed pervasive the notion of the kingdom was to apostolic preaching.

We are looking for passages which set out those things which are essential for those who would have Jesus be their Christ, and there are a few such passages. Most of the cases speak of people being "in Christ", which is where all the spiritual blessings are (Ephesians 1.3-2.10). The only thing which is said to put someone "into Christ" is baptism (Romans 6.1-4, Galatians 3.27), and baptism turns out to be a commitment to live a new life to God (Romans 6.5-11; cf. 2 Corinthians 5.17). In fact, according to Paul, for one truthfully to say he belongs to Christ, not only was it necessary that Christ have died for him, but also that he had been baptized in the name of Christ (1 Corinthians 1.11-13).

An especially interesting passage is Romans 8.1-11:

There is therefore now no condemnation for those who are in Christ Jesus. For the law of the Spirit of life has set you free in Christ Jesus from the law of sin and death. For God has done what the law, weakened by the flesh, could not do. By sending his own Son in the likeness of sinful flesh and for sin, he condemned sin in the flesh, in order that the righteous requirement of the law might be fulfilled in us, who walk not according to the flesh but according to the Spirit. For those who live according to the flesh set their minds on the things of the flesh, but those who live according to the Spirit set their minds on the things of the Spirit. For to set the mind on the flesh is death, but to set the mind on the Spirit is life and peace. For the mind that is set on the flesh is hostile to God, for it does not submit to God's law; indeed, it cannot. Those who are in the flesh cannot please God.

You, however, are not in the flesh but in the Spirit, if in fact the Spirit of God dwells in you. Anyone who does not have the Spirit of Christ does not belong to him. But if Christ is in you, although the body is dead because of sin, the Spirit is life because of righteousness. If the Spirit of him who raised Jesus from the dead dwells in you, he who raised Christ Jesus from the dead will also give life to your mortal bodies through his Spirit who dwells in you.

This passage is all about having the mind of Christ ("spirit" should not be capitalized in these paragraphs). Those who are "in Christ Jesus", that is, have Jesus as their king, live not according to flesh but according to spirit. They set their minds not on things having to do with flesh but rather on things having to do with spirit. They have a submissive attitude toward God's commandments (there is, after all, a law of Christ, 1 Corinthians 9.21, Galatians 6.2). They have the mind of God, which is the mind of Christ, which is to have Christ in them, which is to live in righteousness. The mind of Christ is an attitude which is spiritual enough to accept a crucified Messiah (1 Corinthians 2.1-16) and to live a cruciform life of humble submission to God's will (Philippians 2.1-11).

Accepting Jesus as the Christ is a commitment to a life of obedience to the king. Every thought, in fact, is to be made captive to the obedience of Christ (2 Corinthians 10.5). Christians will be judged by the Christ (Romans 14.9-12, 2 Corinthians 5.10). Paul explicitly mentions the inappropriateness of Christians, whose bodies are members of Christ, engaging their bodies in fornication, which, in the case of the Corinthian Christians, would include every imaginable type of illicit sexual activity (1 Corinthians 6.15-16). And being a stumbling block was also mentioned, which constituted sinning against Christ (1 Corinthians 8.12).

The Son of God

Secondly, as we just saw, the concept of the son of God can easily be associated with the Messiah, or Christ. Though not everyone who might be called a son of a god would also be regarded as a king (cf. Matthew 27.54.), it was often the case that kings were regarded as sons of gods. Nathan the prophet told David that his descendant would sit on his throne and would be a son of God (2 Samuel 7.7-12). The well-known Psalm 2 ("You are my son. Today I have begotten you.") is a coronation psalm (cf. Hebrews 1.5). The coin which Jesus held up in plain view when he discussed paying taxes to Caesar (Matthew 23.15-22, Mark 12.13-17, Luke 20.20-26) was a Roman denarius, which had on its face CAESARUS AUGUSTUS and on the reverse DEUS FILIUS (Son of God). The Jews of Jesus' day certainly used the term with royal significance (Matthew 16.16, 26.63, Mark 14.61, Luke 22.67). And as we saw in Hebrews 1, the title of son was closely aligned with kingship. Furthermore, the appellation "son of David" would also clearly be a designation of kingship (Matthew 21.9, Mark 11.10, Luke 19.34).

There are a great many such ascriptions to Jesus in the New Testament writings. When Saul, the persecutor of Christians, converted, he proclaimed Jesus to be the Son of God (Acts 9.20). Demons called Jesus the Son of God, so did the biblical writers themselves, and the ascription was a matter of debate among both the people and Jesus' enemies.

Since Son of God equals King, the main point is that when people come to regard Jesus as the Son of God, they are committing themselves to obedience to him. When God Himself confirmed Jesus' authority on the Mount of Transfiguration, the injunction to the disciples was to "listen to him", even over Moses (Matthew 17.5, Mark 9.7, Luke 9.35). However, about the only statements we find which tell us what that obedience entails can be found in the Book of Hebrews and in the Epistles of John. In Hebrews 6, the recipients of the writing are warned not to turn away from the faith; to do so would amount to crucifying the Son of God again (6.6; cf. 10.29). In 1 John the writer states that the reason the Son of God was manifested was to destroy sin, and those who have been born of God resist sin and love their spiritual brothers (3.4-10): "And this is his commandment, that we believe in the name of his Son Jesus Christ and love one another, just as he has commanded us" (1 John 3.23; cf. 4.15, 5.6-12).

And of course, there is the famous statement, "Now Jesus did many other signs in the presence of the disciples, which are not written in this book; but these are written so that you may believe that Jesus is the Christ, the Son of God, and that by believing you may have life in his name" (John 20.30-31).

Seated at the Right Hand of God

We now consider a third term. As it has been seen in many passages already cited with regard to Jesus' kingly rule, the term "right hand" is used to refer to Jesus' position over God's kingdom. As far as we know, Jesus himself was the first to apply Psalm 110 to himself as the Messiah:

> Now while the Pharisees were gathered together, Jesus asked them a question, saying, "What do you think about the Christ? Whose son is he?" They said to him, "The son of David." He said to them, "How is it then that David, in the Spirit, calls him Lord, saying,
>> "'The Lord said to my Lord,
>> "Sit at my right hand,
>> until I put your enemies under your feet"'?
> If then David calls him Lord, how is he his son?"

Every anointed Jewish king in the Old Testament was a messiah, so this was not an unusual concept. Jesus, of course, was intimating that he, as the Messiah, was greater than even David (Matthew 22.41-45, cf. Luke 20.41-44). That was an unusual concept.

A similar thing happened in the Sanhedrin:

> But Jesus remained silent. And the high priest said to him, "I adjure you by the living God, tell us if you are the Christ, the Son of God." Jesus said to him, "You have said so. But I tell you, from now on you will see the Son of Man seated at the right hand of Power and coming on the clouds of heaven."

So, Jesus claimed to be the Messiah, the Son of God and seated at the right hand of God (Matthew 26.63-64; cf. Mark 14.61-62, Luke 22.67-69).

A staple of apostolic preaching was that, upon his resurrection from the dead, Jesus ascended to heaven to be seated at the right hand of God and was thus the Messiah, reigning in heaven. This was the conclusion of the first full gospel sermon (Acts 2.1ff.), and the hearers were called upon to repent and be baptized in the name of Jesus the Messiah for the remission of sins. When Stephen was being killed by the hostile crowd, he revealed to them his dying vision of Jesus standing at the right hand of God (Acts 7.54-56). And other writers in the New Testament, as we have already seen, when praising Jesus for his lofty position as the king of God's eternal, spiritual kingdom, made reference to his place at the right hand of God (Romans 8.34, Ephesians 1.20, Hebrews 1.3, 13, 8.1, 10.12, 12.2 and 1 Peter 3.22).

However, as lofty and as inspiring as these passages are, none of them tells us what the implications for kingdom living would be. That makes Colossians 3.1-17 of particular interest:

> If then you have been raised with Christ, seek the things that are above, where Christ is, seated at the right hand of God. Set your minds on things that are above, not on things that are on earth. For you have died, and your life is hidden with Christ in God. When Christ who is your life appears, then you also will appear with him in glory.
>
> Put to death therefore what is earthly in you: sexual immorality, impurity, passion, evil desire, and covetousness, which is idolatry. On account of these the

wrath of God is coming. In these you too once walked, when you were living in them. But now you must put them all away: anger, wrath, malice, slander, and obscene talk from your mouth. Do not lie to one another, seeing that you have put off the old self with its practices and have put on the new self, which is being renewed in knowledge after the image of its creator. Here there is not Greek and Jew, circumcised and uncircumcised, barbarian, Scythian, slave, free; but Christ is all, and in all.

Put on then, as God's chosen ones, holy and beloved, compassionate hearts, kindness, humility, meekness, and patience, bearing with one another and, if one has a complaint against another, forgiving each other; as the Lord has forgiven you, so you also must forgive. And above all these put on love, which binds everything together in perfect harmony. And let the peace of Christ rule in your hearts, to which indeed you were called in one body. And be thankful. Let the word of Christ dwell in you richly, teaching and admonishing one another in all wisdom, singing psalms and hymns and spiritual songs, with thankfulness in your hearts to God. And whatever you do, in word or deed, do everything in the name of the Lord Jesus, giving thanks to God the Father through him.

As with some of the kingdom passages, Paul makes a list of things that are earthly versus things which are "above". Paul draws a distinction between things that are on earth and things that are above, "where Christ is seated at the right hand of God." Once again we find that the characteristics of Jesus' kingdom are spiritual as opposed to those non-kingdom characteristics, which are earthly. This is the flesh/spirit dichotomy again; the above/earthly phrase is just that same dichotomy. So, in the paragraphs that follow, Paul is showing that the nature of the kingdom compels one to place his mind on spiritual things as opposed to allowing his mind to be consumed with the things of the flesh. Both negative as well as positive aspects are listed.

Love binds all the spiritual things together, says Paul. That certainly sounds like Jesus. Jesus' brother James said this (James 2.5):

"Listen, my beloved brothers, has not God chosen those who are poor in the world to be rich in faith and heirs of the kingdom, which he has promised to those who love him?" This statement comes in a context where certain disciples were discriminating between the rich and the poor. Later, in vs. 8, James reminds them that one is to love his neighbor as himself, and he calls this the "royal law". The word "royal" is a kingdom term. So, from this we conclude that to be in the kingdom is to love God and to love one's neighbor. This should come as no surprise, since Jesus told the young lawyer who came to him that living by these two commandments was a part of the kingdom (Matthew 22.34-40, Mark 12.28-34). In fact, the parallels between Jesus' teachings and items from the Book of James (probably Jesus' brother) have often been noted.

Throne

If "right hand" is a kingdom word, then so also would be the word "throne" (cf. Colossians 1.9-20 and Hebrews 1.1-14). Again, as has happened so many times before, we are led to the passage with Jesus and the rich young ruler (Matthew 19.16-30). There Jesus mentioned his throne in conjunction with the kingdom, as well as the thrones of the Twelve. The throne is also mentioned in the parable of the sheep and the goats (Matthew 25.31-46). In Gabriel's announcement to Mary we came across a reference to Jesus assuming David's throne as the son of God, reigning forever over all other thrones, with no end to his kingdom (Luke 1.31-33). Hebrews 4.1-4 has Jesus, the high priest, having passed through the heavens after his resurrection, seated on his throne as the son of God "at the right hand of the throne of the Majesty" (8.1, cf. 12.1-3). The Book of Revelation, of course, has a great deal of throne imagery. In one of the visions of the book, Jesus says, "The one who conquers, I will grant him to sit with me on my throne, as I also conquered and sat down with my Father on his throne." (3.21, cf. 22.1-5). Conquering, according to the Book of Revelation, is staying faithful, even unto death (cf. 20.4-6). So from this we continue to see the emphasis the New Testament places on the kingdom, but also, with throne imagery, we see that those who stayed faithful to the gospel could expect to reign together with Jesus and the Father on His throne.

Lord and Servant

Next, we come to the word "lord", which basically means sir, or master. Just as one can see from comparing the gospels of Matthew and Mark, certain Hebrew concepts had to be reinterpreted to a Gentile audience. So also, the word "Messiah", or "Christ", had to be translated to a Gentile audience. The word used was most often "lord". In Acts 2.36, where Peter enjoined upon his audience to accept the resurrected Jesus as "both lord and Christ", the Jews in his audience would readily understand what the Messiah was but the Gentiles would better understand the word "lord". In one of the few summary passages in the New Testament with regard to the essentials of the gospel, Acts 10.34-43 (cf. 1 Corinthians 15.1-8) Peter makes the basic claim about Jesus, "He is lord of all." Paul would later say that Christ died and lived again in order that he might be lord over the dead and the living (Romans 14.9). That is why Paul preached Jesus the Messiah as lord (2 Corinthians 4.5-6). Not only in these but also in other verses do we find lord used in connection with the kingdom and with other kingdom terms (egs., Matthew 18.23-32, 24.45-51, 25.14-30).

Here are a few representative examples of how "lord" is used in the New Testament. (As a rule, if a verse about lordship has already been discussed in this book, I will omit it here.) In the Sermon on the Mount again, in Matthew 6.24, Jesus punctuated the theme of his kingdom message with the conclusion that "No one can serve two masters (lords). For either he will hate the one and love the other, or he will cling to one and disregard the other. You cannot serve both God and mammon." This really amounts to an antithesis between flesh and spirit. And this is our point in this chapter. Words like "lord" are used in a kingdom sense and carry the same implications as does the word "kingdom". We are reminded of the encounter between Jesus and the rich young ruler. There the issue was, as here, an issue between flesh and spirit, mammon and God. Even when these alternate words for the kingdom are used, the issue invariably comes down to the same thing.

Again in the Sermon on the Mount, there is the statement in 7.21 that one might merely profess submission to Jesus' lordship but not be obedient. Later, "Why do you call me lord, lord and do not do the things I command you?" Jesus asked rhetorically (Luke 6.46-49). In Matthew

10.24-25, Jesus said, "A disciple is not above his teacher, nor a servant above his master. It is enough for the disciple to be like his teacher, and the servant like his master. If they have called the master of the house Beelzebul, how much more will they malign those of his household?" Hence, discipleship and servanthood to Jesus entail seeking to be like Jesus. Similarly, in the Last Supper episode in John 13.12-20, the writer has Jesus saying, "You call me Teacher and Lord, and you are right, for so I am. If I then, your Lord and Teacher, have washed your feet, you also ought to wash one another's feet. For I have given you an example, that you also should do just as I have done to you." Jesus performed an act of servanthood for his disciples which was not required of a rabbi's disciples in that day. If their lord and rabbi was doing the lowly task of washing his disciples' feet, then they should wash one another's.

Let's now go to Paul. Paul uttered that famous phrase, "Because if you confess with your mouth that Jesus is lord and believe in your heart that God raised him from the dead you shall be saved" (Romans 10.9-10). Acknowledging the lordship of Jesus is therefore a step toward salvation. Paul also referred to the Lord's Supper and said that one's participation in that precludes his participation in idolatry: "you cannot drink the cup of the lord and of demons" (I Corinthians 10.21-22). Even earlier he had told the same group of Christ followers that, even though for many people there are many lords, for them there was only one, namely Jesus (1 Corinthians 8.1-4; cf. 2 Corinthians 6.14-7.1, Ephesians 4.5).

We find a picture of despite for lordship authority in 2 Peter 2. The false teachers with whom the author was concerned sought to turn the disciples away from the known way of righteousness, the holy commandment (vs. 21), the right way (vs. 15), by falsely promising them freedom (vs. 19) and urging them to follow their passions (vs. vv. 9-10) and pursue licentiousness (vv. 2, 18).

Now, if lordship is the dominant side of the relationship, then servanthood is the submissive side. Of course, the word "servant", or "slave", occurs many times in the New Testament in the ordinary sense of an earthly slave serving his earthly master, but it is also used in the spiritual sense of a servant of the Lord Messiah Jesus, as we saw above in the "servant not above his master" passages. Servant statements are quite pervasive in the teachings of Jesus, especially in his parables.

Most of the parables about servanthood can be found under the sections on the kingdom, but here is one which is not:

> Will any one of you who has a servant plowing or keeping sheep say to him when he has come in from the field, "Come at once and recline at table"? Will he not rather say to him, "Prepare supper for me, and dress properly, and serve me while I eat and drink, and afterward you will eat and drink"? Does he thank the servant because he did what was commanded? So you also, when you have done all that you were commanded, say, "We are unworthy servants; we have only done what was our duty" (Luke 17.7-10).

This parable has created a great deal of consternation, but the point is that a faithful servant's attitude is submissive. He knows that he owes his master complete obedience and that he has nothing to offer in addition to his best efforts. So, citizens in the Jesus' kingdom should have an attitude of ultra-compliance.

Paul, who often referred to himself as a servant of Jesus the Messiah (Ephesians 4.12, Philippians 1.1 and Titus 1.1), as well as did others (James 1.1, 2 Peter 1.1 and Jude 1), said the following:

> But thanks be to God, that you who were once slaves of sin have become obedient from the heart to the standard of teaching to which you were committed, and, having been set free from sin, have become slaves of righteousness. I am speaking in human terms, because of your natural limitations. For just as you once yielded your members to impurity and to greater and greater iniquity, so now yield your members to righteousness for sanctification. When you were slaves of sin, you were free in regard to righteousness (Romans 6.17-20).

Perhaps this is one of the greatest lordship passages. Here Paul changes his metaphor from that of resurrection to that of master/slave. By this latter metaphor Paul asserts that when one is baptized he changes lords, from the lordship of sin to the lordship of righteousness.

There is also the attitude of servanthood, best expressed in the Philippians hymn (2.3-8):

> Do nothing out of selfish ambition or vain con-

ceit, but in humility consider others better than your-
selves. Each of you should look not only to your own
interests, but also to the interests of others. Your attitude
should be the same as Christ Jesus:

> Who, being in the very form of God, did not
>> consider equality with God
>> something to be grasped,
> But made himself nothing,
>> taking the very form of a servant,
>> being made in human likeness.
> And being found in appearance as a man,
>> he humbled himself
>> and became obedient to death—
>> even death on a cross.

All of this is reminiscent of statements of Jesus, such as his statement
that whoever would be first must become the servant of all, since the son
of man had come not to be served but to serve and to give his life as a
ransom for many (Mark 10.35-45), or his reminder that he was among
them, not like their Gentile rulers, but as one who serves (Luke 22.24-
30). Jesus is lord. We are his servants. But our lord was the quintes-
sential servant. Therefore, we must be servants.

Finally, from Paul in Galatians 1.10 he says, "For am I now
seeking the approval of man, or of God? Or am I trying to please man?
If I were still trying to please man, I would not be a servant of Christ."
Clearly, the lordship of Christ implies that his servants put his will over
the opinions of men.

So, to summarize the lord/servant relationship, though nothing distinctly different is actually added to the concept of citizenship
in Jesus' kingdom, there are some interesting points of emphasis which
emerge from the perspective of lord and servant. First of all, confession
of Jesus as lord is seen to be an essential step in coming to salvation.
This is a confession of exclusivity; there is only one lord, Jesus the
Messiah; idolatry and polytheism are excluded. This confession of Jesus' lordship mainly means that there should be an intense concern with
obedience. Servants in the kingdom should have a willingly compliant
spirit. They are servants of righteousness. In fact, they are willing to
serve righteousness even to the point of flouting human conventions

– even to the point of persecution. Second only to this emphasis on obedience is the emphasis on putting spirit over flesh. As for specific injunctions, probably because of the concept of servanthood itself, the main emphasis is upon the commitment to serving others, especially one's brothers and sisters in the kingdom. Kingdom people humbly serve.

The Name Which Is Above Every Other Name

We now come to the next alternative kingdom term. Closely tied to the concept of lordship is the idea of the name of Jesus Christ. Consider the following passage from Ephesians 1.19-23:

> . . . and what is the immeasurable greatness of his power toward us who believe, according to the working of his great might that he worked in Christ when he raised him from the dead and seated him at his right hand in the heavenly places, far above all rule and authority and power and dominion, and above every name that is named, not only in this age but also in the one to come. And he put all things under his feet and gave him as head over all things to the church, which is his body, the fullness of him who fills all in all. (Cf. 1 Corinthians 15.24, Philippians 2.9).

The writer of the Book of Hebrews said that Jesus had obtained a more excellent name than that of the angels because he was God's son, the anointed king over God's eternal kingdom (Hebrews 1.5-13). Name was associated with authority. When Peter healed the lame man at the Temple gate, the high priest asked him, "By what power, or in what name, did you do this?" (Acts 4.7). Clearly, to talk about the name of Jesus is to talk about his position: his Messiahship, his throne at the right hand of God, and his superior rule, authority, power and lordship.

It seems, though, that there was a special sense in which Jesus' immediate disciples carried his name. He had warned them that they would be persecuted in his name (Matthew 10.22). He also said they would function as a group in his name, that is, by his authority, and that whatever they might bind or loosen "in his name" would be bound and loosened in heaven (Matthew 18.18-20). When they went out to preach, they found that the demons were subject to them in the name of Jesus (Luke 10.17). Jesus also promised them that they would be dragged before kings on account of his name (Luke 21.12). These are hardly things for all disciples in all times. But this is not something new; Jesus elsewhere tells the disciples such things without using the word "name". Furthermore, to say that the Twelve would do such things in his name is not to make those things universal for all disciples; for that to happen we would need statements to the effect that bearing Jesus' name requires, or entails, those things. To those kinds of statements we now turn.

When Jesus sent his immediate disciples out, one of the things they were to do was to make disciples by baptizing people of all nations into the name of the Father, and of the Son and of the Holy Spirit (Matthew 28.18-20). When referring to evangelism, Paul called it bearing the name to the Gentiles (Acts 9.15). So, a person gets into the name by being baptized (cf. Acts 2.38, 10.48 and 19.5). (Paul later chastised a group in Corinth by telling them that one could properly be baptized only in the name of Jesus, cf. I Corinthians 1.13-15). Jesus warmed the disciples' hearts by telling them that repentance could now be preached to all nations in his name (Luke 24.47). Belief in the name of Jesus would give people the power to become children of God (John 1.12, cf. 1 John 3.23), for there is salvation in no other name under heaven (Acts 4.12). On account of Jesus' name people could receive the forgiveness of their sins (Acts 10.43, 1 John 2.12), or eternal life (John 20.31). And there was an obedience of faith concerning the name of Jesus (Romans 1.5). Paul said, "Let everyone who names the name of the Lord depart from iniquity" (2 Timothy 2.19). Suffering was also often associated with bearing the name of Christ (Acts 5.41, 15.66, 1 Peter 4.14). The persecuted disciples in the Book of Revelation bore up through the name of Jesus (2.3, 13). As we saw earlier, Philip preached to the Samaritans concerning the kingdom of God and the name of Jesus the Messiah (Acts 8.12). Paul told the Corinthian disciples that they had been washed, justified and sanctified in the name of the Lord Jesus (1 Corinthians 6.11). So, the name of Jesus is virtually equivalent to the characteristics of the kingdom, as well as to salvation terms.

There is another phrase, "calling on the name of the lord", which is relevant at this point. It is an Old Testament phrase which means to put one's trust in the Lord (cf. Joel 2.32 and 3.5). In Acts 2, after Peter had established that Jesus was "both Lord and Christ", he exhorted his listeners to call upon the name of the lord in order to be saved (vs. 21; cf. Romans 10.1-17), and this just after he had told them to repent and be baptized in the name of Jesus the Messiah (vs. 38). The first act of obedience to the gospel was, in fact, to be baptized. Ananias said to Paul, "Why do you tarry? Arise and get yourself baptized, and wash away your sins, calling on the name of the lord" (Acts 22.16). Those who followed Jesus were said to be those who called upon the name of the lord (Acts 9.14, 21 and 1 Corinthians 1.2). Finally, Paul told Timothy, "So flee youthful passions and pursue righteousness, faith, love, and peace, along with those who call on the Lord from a pure heart "(2 Ti 2.22).

To summarize the idea of the name of the Lord Jesus, perhaps the main thing is that Jesus' name is superior to every other name which can be named. In that name one can find salvation, which is accessed through faith, repentance and baptism. One continues to call upon the name of Jesus by following the principles of righteous living.

Authority and Submission

Let us now take up the word "authority". It has already appeared in our study in groupings with kingdom, rule, name, etc. (Matthew 21.23-22.14, 1 Corinthians 15.24, Ephesians 1.20-23, Colossians 1.9-20, 1 Peter 3.22). In the gospels, a great deal of emphasis is placed on the authority of Jesus. Jesus taught with authority (Matthew 7.29). He claimed to have authority on earth to forgive sins (Matthew 9.6-8, Mark 2.1-16, Luke 5.17-26). In Jesus' well-known prayer in John 17.1ff., Jesus acknowledged that God the Father had given him authority over all flesh to give eternal life to human beings. And as these would suggest, Jesus' authority was from God (Matthew 21.23-27, Mark 11.27-33, Luke 20.1-8, John 5.16-47). Later, the Twelve and other leaders claimed this authority. But let's see what Jesus' authority implies for those under his authority.

First of all, under the rubric of authority, there is the Great Commission (Matthew 28.18-20):

And Jesus came and said to them, "All authority in heaven and on earth has been given to me. Go therefore and make disciples of all nations, baptizing them in

the name of the Father and of the Son and of the Holy
Spirit, teaching them to observe all that I have commanded you. And behold, I am with you always, to the
end of the age."

This passage has been called up before, when we considered one's being
baptized into the name. But though there is no mention of the kingdom
here, Jesus is claiming universal authority, reminiscent of the lofty passages elsewhere in the New Testament which assert Jesus' superiority
over all types of rulers everywhere. This passage, then, would make
evangelism a universal characteristic of Jesus' kingdom.

Similarly, Paul testified to Agrippa that Jesus had sent him to
the Gentiles " to open their eyes, so that they may turn from darkness to
light and from the power (authority) of Satan to God, that they may receive forgiveness of sins and a place among those who are sanctified by
faith in (him)" (Acts 26.15-18). This is very much like his statement in
Colossians in which he mentioned being transferred from the kingdom
of darkness to the kingdom of God's dear son (1.11-16; cf. Ephesians
2.2). The concept of authority, therefore, is the same as the concept of
the kingdom. To the king, Paul went on to say, " "Therefore, O King
Agrippa, I was not disobedient to the heavenly vision, but declared first
to those in Damascus, then in Jerusalem and throughout all the region
of Judea, and also to the Gentiles, that they should repent and turn to
God, performing deeds in keeping with their repentance" (vv. 19-20).
So, to submit to the authority (kingly rule) of Christ involved, for Paul,
repentance, turning to God and living a life of repentance. These can
be seen to be three distinct things, since clearly the works are a result of
repentance and are not identical with repentance itself. Repentance is a
profound commitment to turn one's life over to God's authority. Turning to God in the Book of Acts occurred at the point of baptism (compare Acts 2.38 with 3.19). Then, of course, the life of works followed.

The flip side of authority is submission, or subjection:

For those who live according to the flesh set their
minds on the things of the flesh, but those who live according to the Spirit set their minds on the things of the
Spirit. To set the mind on the flesh is death, but to set
the mind on the Spirit is life and peace. For the mind that
is set on the flesh is hostile to God; it does not submit

to God's law, indeed it cannot; and those who are in the flesh cannot please God (Romans 8.5-8).

Power

Let's take up the concept of Jesus' power next. We have already seen how Jesus' power is a kingdom term (Acts 4.7, Matthew 26.64, Mark 14.62, Luke 4.36, 22.69, Romans 1.4, 1 Corinthians 15.24, Ephesians 1.21, Colossians 1.9-20, 1 Peter 3.22). It is especially closely associated with authority (Luke 4.36, 5.17 and 10.17; also name Acts 4.7, 1 Corinthians 5.3-5 and also son of God, Romans 1.4). But Matthew 24.30 is especially expressive, where it says that the son of man would return "upon the clouds of heaven with power and great glory" (cf. Matthew 26.64, Mark 13.26, 14.62, Luke 21.27, 22.69). To the elect, Jesus is the power of God (1 Corinthians 1.24). Finally, the Twelve received "power from on high", which placed them in the position of authority and put them in the company of the "witnesses" (Luke 24.49, Acts 1.8). That said, however, there are no statements in connection with the power of Jesus that would indicate any requirements on the parts of citizens of Jesus' kingdom.

Head

The concept of headship would also be a kingdom term. In Colossians 2.6-15 there is a clear connection: Jesus is lord, he is the head of all rule and authority, and he has triumphed over all principalities and powers. The disciples in Colossae, as a result of their faith in Jesus, their repentance and baptism, had been forgiven of their sins, had been resurrected from their spiritual death and had come to fullness of life in Jesus. However, Jesus' headship is usually connected to the church (Ephesians 1.22, 4.15, 5.23, Colossians 1.18). Though it is a difficult topic, we would argue that the church is part of the kingdom and not identical with it. So, in 1 Corinthians 11.1-11, where it says that God is the head of Christ, Christ is the head of the man and the man is the head of the woman, that could be a statement about the church in Paul's time and not a kingdom principle. It's not clear.

Ruler

Finally, the word "ruler" is applied sometimes to Satan as the ruler of demons (Matthew 9.34, 12.24, Mark 3.22, 11.15, John 12.31, 42, 14.30, 16.11). Otherwise, it refers to human rulers. The passage in Ephesians 1, which we have quoted and referred to several times, has Jesus above all rulers. This would probably include Satan and all earthly rulers (cf. Revelation 1.5).

Conclusion

This has been a fast-paced and lengthy look at alternative terms for kingdom. Two main things emerge. First, the variety of kingdom terms shows once again how dominant the kingdom idea really is in the gospel. It's all about the kingdom. The reader might be tempted to say that The Kingdom Algorithm gets us back to the whole New Testament, and that's almost true. But there are still many passages which would by the algorithm be understood as applying to the early disciples and not to us. But once again, the idea of the kingdom is central.

Secondly, not only are the rewards, such as forgiveness and eternal life, the same, but the requirements of the kingdom, no matter what term is used to refer to it, remain the same. Faith, repentance and baptism put one into the kingdom. Jesus as Lord requires thorough-going obedience, even the mind being captive to obedience. Mainly obedience is about putting spirit over flesh, and the list from Colossians 3, which details that distinction, is similar to the ones we saw under the kingdom. Of course, loving the brothers is especially emphasized. Those who bear the name of Christ also set out to imitate the master in his character, and especially with regard to his humble servanthood. Finally, there must also be a commitment which extends even to the point of suffering and death. To fall away from the faith, even under the pressure of persecution, is to leave the kingdom.

7 Testing The Algorithm

We think we have an algorithm for applying the Bible to our lives today. It is as follows: if the scriptures set forth something as essential to the kingdom of Christ, then that is to be applied universally; otherwise not. We have surveyed the New Testament for these conditions, taking into account kingdom cognates as well. But in this chapter we propose a test. People would want to be in the Kingdom of Christ because of what it affords, namely salvation, eternal life, etc. Let's survey those terms, as well, to see if the same conditions prevail. If we were to find that some of the things explicitly stated in the scriptures to be necessary for salvation were not explicitly stated to be necessary for entrance into the kingdom, then that would militate against the centrality of the kingdom. However, if one enters the kingdom in order to receive eternal life, and if indeed the conditions for receiving eternal life are the same as the conditions to enter the kingdom, then that would mean that we are on the right track.

Allow us to put that another way. Suppose someone were to ask why the kingdom of God should be the central paradigm in reading and applying the Bible to our lives. There are other candidates for that position, certainly. For example, salvation, or eternal life. Our questioner might continue by suggesting that, if we are indeed saddled with the necessity of using an algorithm in order to be consistent, why we shouldn't make salvation the basis of an algorithm. Our response is that we think that that is a very good question, and it gives rise to a test, an experiment, if you will, to see if the kingdom algorithm is correct. Let's accumulate all the salvation terms we can find and the conditions mentioned in the New Testament for gaining salvation. If the list of conditions for salvation is markedly different from the list of conditions for entering the kingdom, then it would seem that something is awry with The Kingdom Algorithm.

The Blessings of the Kingdom

In a story we discussed earlier, the rich young ruler (Matthew 19.16-30, cf. Mark 10.17-31, Luke 18.18-30) asked Jesus, "Teacher, what good deed must I do, to have eternal life?" But when Jesus' answer disappointed the young man and he went away sorrowful, Jesus remarked how hard it would be for those with riches "to enter the kingdom of heaven". In fact, in this same account, Jesus and his disciples use other terms in close conjunction with the word "kingdom". Jesus told the young man that by keeping the commandments he could "enter life". He then told the young man that he could have "treasure in heaven". But then Jesus' amazed disciples asked, "Who then can be saved?" Jesus then answered his disciples' question by referring to his kingdom as "the new world" (or "regeneration") and promising all who left family and homes for the sake of the kingdom a reward, including eternal life. In order for the conversation in this gospel episode to work, all of these terms must be viewed as very closely related.

But in addition to the story of the rich young ruler, there are many passages in the rest of the New Testament which connect citizenship in the kingdom of God with other salvation-type terms. The Beatitudes equate the following:

Citizenship in the kingdom of heaven
Comfort from bearing one's sins
Inheriting the land (the new world, cf. Matthew 19.28 and comp. Luke 22.28-30)

Satisfaction in one's desire for righteousness, that is, justification

Mercy, forgiveness

A relationship with God

From the rest of the Sermon on the Mount, as well as the whole of the sermon's flip side, Matthew 23, Jesus' kingdom was for those who wished to attain life, instead of destruction in hell (Mathew 5.29-30, 7.13-14, 25.41, 46, Luke 21.19), for those who wished to be saved (cf. Mathew 19.28, 24.22, Mark 13.20) instead of experiencing God's judgment (Mathew 5.22), as well as for those who sought forgiveness (Mathew 6.14-15). In the kingdom one could enjoy a reward in heaven (Matthew 5.12, 6.4, 6) and could store up treasures in heaven (Mathew 6.19-21).

In the remainder of the gospels, there are many other connections between the kingdom and salvation terms. In the parables section, the metaphor of the kingdom of God conjures up the mental picture of a city of light atop a hill in the night (cf. Matthew 5.14). Those inside the walls are safe and secure, while those outside will be thrown in a furnace of fire (Matthew 13.36-43). Later, Jesus said that as king he would one day storm the city of death, break down its gates and despoil it of its righteous holdings, in other words, he would raise the righteous dead. Also, as Messiah, he gave the Twelve the power to forgive sins (Matthew 16.13-20). And, in the Olivet Discourse, the king dispenses eternal life and eternal judgment (Mathew 25.31-46; cf. Matthew 3.11-12, Mark 1.7-8, Luke 3.15-18)

In the Book of Acts, Paul preached the gospel to the Jews in Jerusalem, testifying that in the kingdom of God one could find salvation (Acts 28.23-29).

But turning to Paul's writings themselves, we find Paul saying that in the kingdom one can rejoice in the washing away of sins, sanctification and justification (1 Corinthians 6.9-11), also immortality (1 Corinthians 15.50-57). Spirituality, as opposed to fleshliness, is essential to one's citizenship in the kingdom of God, and the spiritual shall gain immortality, as opposed to corruption (Galatians 5.16-6.10). Those outside the kingdom would experience the wrath of God (Ephesians 5.5-6), but those in the kingdom of light are in Christ, where they receive redemption and the forgiveness of sins (Colossians 1.13-14).

The kingdom which cannot be shaken, according to Hebrews 12.18-29, is the city of the living God, the assembly of the first-born who are enrolled in heaven and the spirits of just men made perfect.

Finally, in the Book of Revelation, the kingdom is made up of those who had been freed from their sins by the blood of Jesus (1.5-6), those who have been ransomed by Jesus' blood (5.9-10), those reigning with Christ in the resurrection (20.4-6) and those who are called sons of God (21.1-22.5, esp. 21.7).

Here, then, from the New Testament, are the blessings of kingdom citizenship:

> forgiveness of sins,
> washing away of sins,
> freed from sins by the blood of Jesus,
> justification,
> sanctification,
> redemption,
> a relationship with God,
> sonship of God,
> life,
> eternal life,
> immortality,
> salvation,
> reward in heaven,
> treasures in heaven,
> resurrection, and
> reigning with Christ.

It turns out, then, at first blush that the blessings of being in the kingdom are in fact salvation, forgiveness, eternal life and all the other salvation-like things (we'll call this the salvation nexus) we find in the gospel. But our experiment is far from being completely run. We now want to find in the New Testament, ignoring all of the kingdom passages, all the conditions for the salvation nexus and compare them with the conditions for being in the kingdom. Again, if the algorithm were to be extended to include all of these additional aspects and we got the same results, then that would be an indication that that the algorithm gives us what is required of all citizens of Jesus' kingdom for all times in all provinces and in all cultures. We will be moving through these passages quickly, without much commentary.

The Conditions of Salvation

First of all, there is a condition very close to humility, discussed above, and that concept is the willingness of a person to open his eyes and ears to the message of the gospel. Jesus said, "Truly, truly, I say to you, whoever hears my word and believes him who sent me has eternal life. He does not come into judgment, but has passed from death to life" (John 5.24). Similarly, in the Good Shepherd passage, Jesus said, "My sheep hear my voice, and I know them, and they follow me. I give them eternal life, and they will never perish, and no one will snatch them out of my hand." (John 10.27-28; cf. 9.39-41). In the Book of Acts, there is a message which saves people (11.14), and Paul said that he was sent especially to the Gentiles "to open their eyes, so that they may turn from darkness to light and from the power of Satan to God, that they may receive forgiveness of sins and a place among those who are sanctified by faith in (Jesus)'" (26.18). None of these passages mentions the kingdom of God, yet the blessings of the kingdom are still there.

The next condition is to believe, accept or receive, the gospel. This involves seeing the gospel as the truth. Paul said that the Thessalonians had been sanctified and saved by their belief in the truth (2 Thessalonians 2.13-14). Just as Jesus said that knowing the truth set one free (John 8.31-32), Paul said that the truth helps one escape the snare of the Devil (2 Timothy 2.24-26) and that refusing to love the truth would get in the way of a person's being saved (2 Thessalonians 2.9-12; cf. John 6.50-58, 63, Acts 13.46-47, 18.6).

Believing also involves believing in the one true Creator God, the God of Abraham, Isaac and Jacob. Hebrews 11:6: "And without faith it is impossible to please him, for whoever would draw near to God must believe that he exists and that he rewards those who seek him" (cf. the whole of Hebrews 11 and also 12.25).

The condition of faith also includes believing in Jesus. Jesus said, "For God so loved the world, that he gave his only Son, that whoever believes in him should not perish but have eternal life" (John 3.16). The Beloved Disciple said that by believing that Jesus is the Messiah, the Son of God, the believer might have life in Jesus' name (John 20.30-31). Believing in Jesus gives one the power to become a child of God (John 1.12). Peter said, "To (Jesus) all the prophets bear witness that everyone who believes in him receives forgiveness of sins through his name" (Acts 10.43). And Paul said that people believe in Jesus for eternal life (I Timothy 1.16). There are so many non-kingdom passages about believing in Jesus (cf. John 6.40, 47, 11.25-26, Acts 5.14, 13.38-39, 16.30-3, Galatians 3.25-29, I John 5.1,13).

Finally, belief involves believing the gospel message about what God did for humankind through Jesus, for example, "And he said to them, 'Go into all the world and proclaim the gospel to the whole creation. Whoever believes and is baptized will be saved, but whoever does not believe will be condemned" (Mark 16.15-16; cf. John 4.13-14, Romans 1.16, 10.9, 1 Thessalonians 4.13-14). So, faith is a condition necessary to receiving these kingdom blessings, even though in the above verses the kingdom is not mentioned.

According to the New Testament writers, persons can believe the gospel but still not be in a saved condition. James made this point the clearest when he compared inactive believers to demons: "You believe that God is one; you do well. Even the demons believe — and shudder!" (James 2.19b). "Jesus said to the Jews who had believed him, 'If you abide in my word, you are truly my disciples, and you will know the truth, and the truth will set you free'" (John 8.31-32). Obviously, those believing Jews to whom Jesus was speaking were still not free from their sins. This is similar to John 12.41-50:

> Nevertheless, many even of the authorities believed in him, but for fear of the Pharisees they did not confess it, so that they would not be put out of the synagogue; for they loved the glory that comes from man more than the glory that comes from God.
>
> And Jesus cried out and said, "Whoever believes in me, believes not in me but in him who sent me. And whoever sees me sees him who sent me. I have come into the world as light, so that whoever believes in me may not remain in darkness. If anyone hears my words

and does not keep them, I do not judge him; for I did not come to judge the world but to save the world. The one who rejects me and does not receive my words has a judge; the word that I have spoken will judge him on the last day. For I have not spoken on my own authority, but the Father who sent me has himself given me a commandment—what to say and what to speak. And I know that his commandment is eternal life. What I say, therefore, I say as the Father has told me."

Even if a person believed in Jesus, though that belief was a necessary condition of their salvation, it was still not sufficient for them to escape judgment. And according to the introduction to the Fourth Gospel, belief in Jesus gives one the power to become a child of God (John 1.12), leaving it open as to whether the believer would execute that power.

Now, according to the New Testament, the essential motivating factor for faith to become active is love: love for God, love for Jesus and love for the word. This love for God and the gospel is really based on an appreciation of God's grace (Acts 15.11, Romans 4.1-8, 5.12-21, Ephesians 2.1-10) and is essential to salvation. Jesus is famous for saying that the main thing one needed to do to inherit eternal life was to love God with his whole heart and to love his neighbor as himself (Luke 10.25-28). Jesus also said, "If anyone loves me, he will keep my word, and my Father will love him, and we will come to him and make our home with him. Whoever does not love me does not keep my words. And the word that you hear is not mine but the Father's who sent me" (John 14.23-24). Paul said, "Henceforth there is laid up for me the crown of righteousness, which the Lord, the righteous judge, will award to me on that Day, and not only to me but also to all who have loved his appearing" (2 Timothy 4.8). He also said that what kept him pushing forward, instead of falling away, was "the surpassing worth of knowing Christ Jesus as Lord" (Philippians 3.8). Further, he said that those who refused to love the truth would not be saved (2 Thessalonians 2.10). And finally, "For in Christ Jesus neither circumcision nor uncircumcision counts for anything, but only faith working through love" (Galatians 5.6). Whether it's fellowship with God and His Son, the crown of eternal life or salvation, all things which one can find in the kingdom, one must love God for what He has done for us in order to gain those things.

So, a person hears the gospel and believes it. He loves the truth of the gospel, and that love for God and what God has done for him motivates him to act upon his faith. The first thing the motivated believer should do is repent. All through the New Testament new believers are told to repent in order that their sins might be forgiven. The first gospel sermon replete with all the elements of the gospel concludes as following, "Repent and be baptized every one of you in the name of Jesus Christ for the forgiveness of your sins, and you will receive the gift of the Holy Spirit" (Acts 2.38; cf. 3.19, 26.15-20). Paul said to his hearers in Athens, "The times of ignorance God overlooked, but now he commands all people everywhere to repent, because he has fixed a day on which he will judge the world in righteousness by a man whom he has appointed; and of this he has given assurance to all by raising him from the dead" (Ac 17.30-31). Paul told Timothy to be kind to his opponents; after all, "God may perhaps grant them repentance leading to a knowledge of the truth, and they may come to their senses and escape from the snare of the devil, after being captured by him to do his will" (2 Timothy 2.24-26). Finally, Peter said, "The Lord is not slow to fulfill his promise as some count slowness, but is patient toward you, not wishing that any should perish, but that all should reach repentance" (2 Peter 3.9).

Baptism turns up again as an important condition of salvation. Baptism was enjoined upon penitent believers for salvation (see Mark 16.15-16, quoted above). Forgiveness of sins is a blessing of kingdom citizenship, and in certain non-kingdom passages baptism is a condition which must be met to receive that blessing. Ananias urged the penitent Saul, "And now why do you wait? Rise and be baptized and wash away your sins, calling on his name" (Acts 22.16; cf. Acts 2.38, quoted above). Later, Saul, now Paul, wrote to the Colossian disciples:

> In him also you were circumcised with a circumcision made without hands, by putting off the body of the flesh, by the circumcision of Christ, having been buried with him in baptism, in which you were also raised with him through faith in the powerful working of God, who raised him from the dead. And you, who were dead in your trespasses and the uncircumcision of your flesh, God made alive together with him, having forgiven us all

our trespasses, by canceling the record of debt that stood against us with its legal demands. This he set aside, nailing it to the cross. He disarmed the rulers and authorities and put them to open shame, by triumphing over them in him" (Colossians 2.11-15).

In Chapter 6 we saw how being in the kingdom puts one in union with Christ, so much so that the kingdom citizen can be said even to reign with Christ. But one gets into Christ through baptism. Romans 6.1-4:

> What shall we say then? Are we to continue in sin that grace may abound? By no means! How can we who died to sin still live in it? Do you not know that all of us who have been baptized into Christ Jesus were baptized into his death? We were buried therefore with him by baptism into death, in order that, just as Christ was raised from the dead by the glory of the Father, we too might walk in newness of life.

And again in Galatians 3.25-29:

> But now that faith has come, we are no longer under a guardian, for in Christ Jesus you are all sons of God, through faith. For as many of you as were baptized into Christ have put on Christ. There is neither Jew nor Greek, there is neither slave nor free, there is no male and female, for you are all one in Christ Jesus. And if you are Christ's, then you are Abraham's offspring, heirs according to promise.

Perhaps the most dramatic statement about baptism is found in 1 Peter 3.21-22: "Baptism, which corresponds to this, now saves you, not as a removal of dirt from the body but as an appeal to God for a good conscience, through the resurrection of Jesus Christ, who has gone into heaven and is at the right hand of God, with angels, authorities, and powers having been subjected to him."

John the Baptizer and Jesus worked together for a while along the Jordan River. During this time, an eminent man by the name of Nicodemus came to Jesus. As we saw in Chapter Three above, in their conversation Jesus enjoined upon Nicodemus the necessity of being born again, but he also styled it being "born of water and Spirit" (John

3.3-5). This is a kingdom passage, since Jesus made the spiritual rebirth of water a condition of the kingdom. Yet, Paul also referred to believers being saved by "the washing of regeneration" in (Titus 3.5-7). We believe that baptism, immersion in water in the name of Jesus Christ for the remission of sins, is the new birth. Baptism is also a way of publically confessing Christ. This confession is necessary to salvation (Romans 10.9-13). So, once again, just as with the kingdom, baptism becomes an important part of God's eternal plan.

There is also a great deal in the New Testament about the necessity of continued discipleship. Jesus said the hour was coming when the dead would be raised, those who had done good to a resurrection of life and those who had done evil to a resurrection of judgment (John 5.25-29). The writer of Hebrews compared their Christian lives at that point in time to the forty years of wandering of the Israelites in the desert. His concern was that the Christians not fall away as did many of the Israelites. Instead, he urged them to strive to enter the Sabbath rest of God (3.12-4.13). Later, the same writer said, "For if we go on sinning deliberately after receiving the knowledge of the truth, there no longer remains a sacrifice for sins, but a fearful expectation of judgment, and a fury of fire that will consume the adversaries" (10.26-27). The reward, he said, is for those who diligently seek God (11.6, quoted above). 1 John 1.5-7 says that disciples need to continue to walk in the light, not in the darkness, in order to stay in fellowship with God. Paul knew that, even after having preached to others, he needed to keep struggling in the faith in order not to be cast away (1 Corinthians 9.24-27; cf. Philippians 3.8-16). Those who continued to pursue spiritual things over the flesh would receive eternal life and not destruction. For example, Paul said this to believers in Galatia:

> Do not be deceived: God is not mocked, for whatever one sows, that will he also reap. For the one who sows to his own flesh will from the flesh reap corruption, but the one who sows to the Spirit will from the Spirit reap eternal life. And let us not grow weary of doing good, for in due season we will reap, if we do not give up (Galatians 6.7-9, cf. Romans 8.5-17).

James said:

> What good is it, my brothers, if someone says he

has faith but does not have works? Can that faith save him? If a brother or sister is poorly clothed and lacking in daily food, and one of you says to them, "Go in peace, be warmed and filled," without giving them the things needed for the body, what good is that?

But someone will say, "You have faith and I have works." Show me your faith apart from your works, and I will show you my faith by my works. You believe that God is one; you do well. Even the demons believe—and shudder! Do you want to be shown, you foolish person, that faith apart from works is useless? Was not Abraham our father justified by works when he offered up his son Isaac on the altar? You see that faith was active along with his works, and faith was completed by his works; and the Scripture was fulfilled that says, "Abraham believed God, and it was counted to him as righteousness"—and he was called a friend of God. You see that a person is justified by works and not by faith alone (Js 2.14-16).

And Paul said something very similar (Philippians 2.12-13), "Therefore, my beloved, as you have always obeyed, so now, not only as in my presence but much more in my absence, work out your own salvation with fear and trembling, for it is God who works in you, both to will and to work for his good pleasure." Continued discipleship was based on staying with the original teachings of Jesus and the apostles. 1 John 2.24-25 says, "Let what you heard from the beginning abide in you. If what you heard from the beginning abides in you, then you too will abide in the Son and in the Father. And this is the promise that he made to us—eternal life." Actually, this is probably what Jesus meant when he said that those who ate his flesh and drank his blood would be raised up on the last day to enjoy eternal life (John 6.53-58); to eat his flesh and drink his blood was to live by his teachings (see our discussion on John 6 in Chapter 3).

Just as we found in our study of the conditions for abiding in the kingdom, not only must we disciples be willing to suffer for the faith, we also need to understand that suffering refines us, with the result that we obtain the salvation of our souls (1Peter 1.3-9). There is a crown of life for those who stand the test (James 1.2-12). God's chastisement is to keep us from being condemned along with the world (1 Corinthians 11.32). As Jesus said, "The one who endures to the end will be saved" (Matthew 24.13, cf. Mark 13.13, Luke 21.19). And standing firm in the face of persecution results in salvation, according to Philippians 1.27-28.

It is clearly taught in the New Testament that saved Christians can fall away and ultimately lose their salvation. For example the preacher in the Book of Hebrews said (Hebrews 6.1-8):

> Therefore let us leave the elementary doctrine of Christ and go on to maturity, not laying again a foundation of repentance from dead works and of faith toward God, and of instruction about washings, the laying on of hands, the resurrection of the dead, and eternal judgment. And this we will do if God permits. For it is impossible, in the case of those who have once been enlightened, who have tasted the heavenly gift, and have shared in the Holy Spirit, and have tasted the goodness of the word of God and the powers of the age to come, and then have fallen away, to restore them again to repentance, since they are crucifying once again the Son of God to their own harm and holding him up to contempt. For land that has drunk the rain that often falls on it, and produces a crop useful to those for whose sake it is cultivated, receives a blessing from God. But if it bears thorns and thistles, it is worthless and near to being cursed, and its end is to be burned.

This graphic language is not nearly as startling as the language we find in 2 Peter 2.20-22:

> For if, after they have escaped the defilements of the world through the knowledge of our Lord and Savior Jesus Christ, they are again entangled in them and overcome, the last state has become worse for them than the first. For it would have been better for them never to have known the way of righteousness than after knowing it to turn back from the holy commandment delivered to them. What the true proverb says has happened to them:

"The dog returns to its own vomit, and the sow, after washing herself, returns to wallow in the mire."

Even Jesus was concerned about his own immediate disciples, the Twelve, not continuing to do what he had commanded them to do. John 15.1-11, records some of his final words to them before the cross:

> I am the true vine, and my Father is the vine-dresser. Every branch in me that does not bear fruit he takes away, and every branch that does bear fruit he prunes, that it may bear more fruit. Already you are clean because of the word that I have spoken to you. Abide in me, and I in you. As the branch cannot bear fruit by itself, unless it abides in the vine, neither can you, unless you abide in me. I am the vine; you are the branches. Whoever abides in me and I in him, he it is that bears much fruit, for apart from me you can do nothing. If anyone does not abide in me he is thrown away like a branch and withers; and the branches are gathered, thrown into the fire, and burned. If you abide in me, and my words abide in you, ask whatever you wish, and it will be done for you. By this my Father is glorified, that you bear much fruit and so prove to be my disciples. As the Father has loved me, so have I loved you. Abide in my love. If you keep my commandments, you will abide in my love, just as I have kept my Father's commandments and abide in his love. These things I have spoken to you, that my joy may be in you, and that your joy may be full.

The figure of burning barren branches is graphic. Jesus seemed to be saying that even some of his closest disciples might be spiritually barren and not be saved.

Paul told the Corinthian Christians to hold on fast to the gospel in order to be saved (1 Corinthians 15.1-2, cf. Colossians 1.21-23). He later told Timothy (2 Timothy 2.11-13):

> The saying is trustworthy, for
>> If we have died with him,
>>> we will also live with him;
>> if we endure, we will also reign with him;

> if we deny him, he also will deny us;
> if we are faithless, he remains faithful—
> for he cannot deny himself.

Christians need to endure the difficulties that come with the kingdom. Failure to do so amounts to denying him. As we've said before, the writer of the Book of Hebrews was concerned that his listeners might abandon the new faith and go back to their ancient roots, Judaism. He encouraged them through examples of steadfastness from the Old Testament. "But we are not of those who shrink back and are destroyed, but of those who have faith and preserve their souls" (Hebrews 10.39). Finally, if a believer brings one back from wanderer away from the truth into error he effectually saves his soul from death (James 5.19-20). So, from all of these statements on endurance it follows that there must be some effort on the part of the disciple of Christ to remain faithful to Christ.

Yet all of this about the required life of discipleship is in general language. The early writers and leaders often attached salvation to some specific behaviors. Above all would be the necessity of having the mind of Christ, that is, having a spiritual attitude, in order to stay in relationship with him (Romans 8.9-11). A great deal of stress is placed on loving our Christian brothers and sisters (especially, the whole book of 1 John). The willingness to confess our faith to the world is a salvation issue; Jesus said, "So everyone who acknowledges me before men, I also will acknowledge before my Father who is in heaven, but whoever denies me before men, I also will deny before my Father who is in heaven" (Matthew 10.32-33; cf. Luke 12.8-9). Other things would include forgiving others; if we do not forgive, we shall not be forgiven (Matthew 18.23-35 and James 2.13). Also, there are these things: being responsible for the care of one's family (1 Timothy 5.7-8), loving one's neighbor (1 Thessalonians 3.11-13) and being careful about one's teaching (1 Timothy 4.16 and 2 John 9).

There are also some specific negatives, prohibitions, which are also tied to salvation. Preaching another gospel will bring a curse upon one's soul (Galatians 1.6-8, 5.4). A person who is stubbornly factious is self-condemned (Titus 3.10-11). No murderer has eternal life abiding in him (1 John 3.15). A disciple who rebels will not escape judgment (Hebrews 12.25, Jude 8-13). And finally, Christians who turn back to a life of sensuality will wind up in a condition worse than if they had never heard the gospel (2 Peter 2.20-22).

Conclusion

The above conditions of salvation, eternal life, forgiveness, etc. are essentially the same conditions we summarized in the last chapters. In order to receive salvation, along with the salvation equivalences, like eternal life and the forgiveness of sins, one needs to be humble and open to the gospel, and upon believing, motivated by love for God and what He has done for her, she needs to repent and be baptized. In order to stay in possession of those salvation qualities, she needs to continue to obey and to grow in her spirituality. She needs to live a life that would glorify God, and she needs to be prepared to endure the struggles that come with discipleship, including persecution. More than anything, she must put spirit over flesh. Certain sins could eventually exclude her from salvation, including obvious ones, like murder, stealing, lying, adultery and factiousness. Correct doctrine is necessary on some level; one can pervert the basic message of the gospel to a degree that it would cut her off from Christ. Finally, in order to stay in God's grace, she must love others, be forgiving and be careful to take care of her closest responsibilities.

But none of this is new. These are the same conditions we found for life in the kingdom and the same conditions we found in the last chapter. In fact, Chapter 6 and this chapter complement each other and, taken together; whether we look at cognates for the kingdom or the rewards of the kingdom, the conditions remain virtually the same. Though one list might sharpen the other, they are basically the same, and this supports our contention that the Kingdom Algorithm is what God would have us use in order to find what principles and practices we are to take away from the Bible and apply to our lives today as Christ followers.

We began this chapter by proposing a test. It was as follows: if we were to make the salvation nexus our paradigm for applying the Bible to our lives and if we, upon examining the New Testament, were to find a list of conditions for gaining salvation which was significantly different from the list of conditions for being in the kingdom, then we would have a big problem. Since salvation might very well claim precedence for being the algorithm we should use for applying the New Testament to our lives, then we would have two competing algorithms, making the whole enterprise appear to be quite hopeless. But as it turns out, not only is the salvation nexus of blessings to be found in the kingdom, but the conditions explicitly stated for gaining them are the same as the conditions for being in the Christ's kingdom, as well as the same conditions we found under the kingdom cognates in Chapter 6. It's all the same thing, in other words. However the kingdom is referred to, it is where we find salvation, and the conditions are all the same. The Kingdom Algorithm, therefore, is the paradigm we should use to apply the teaching of the Bible to our lives today as Christians.

Given that, we want in the next chapter to summarize our findings.

8 The Universal Citizen of the Kingdom of Christ

There is atop the spiritual Mt. Zion, a fortress, gloriously beaming with the light of God's love, the New Jerusalem, the walled city of the Kingdom of God. Inside this city reside God, His Messiah and all of God's people of all ages. This is the Kingdom of God, wherein one can find salvation from sin and eternal life in relationship with the one true God. Outside the city men sit in darkness.

What is Required of All Followers of Christ

This chapter is dedicated to summarizing the findings of the last five. To repeat the algorithm: whatever one finds in the Bible as inextricably essential to the spiritual kingdom of Christ is essential for all Christians for all time; otherwise not. If The Kingdom Algorithm is the way we should approach the Bible today and apply it to our lives, then what are the results of it? We want to answer that question here, and we want to present our findings in a systematic way. (There will be some repetition in the description below, though we have sought to minimize it.) Also, in this chapter we want to set out some rather obvious features of modern Christianity which do not emerge from the implementation of the algorithm as essential aspects of Christianity. So, we start with a depiction of the universal citizen of the kingdom of Christ.

1. Perhaps, because an attitude of openness to truth is psychologically prior to accepting the gospel in the first place, the willingness to accept truth, wherever it might lead, is an absolutely essential prerequisite to citizenship in the kingdom of Christ.

2. The universal citizen of the kingdom of Christ knows who the one true God is: the one and only Creator of the material universe. He also knows God as the God of Abraham, Isaac and Jacob. Because of God being who He is, the kingdom person trusts God over any other source of direction in the world. This belief in the one true God entails the rejection of all other gods and, consequently, the rejection of idolatry.

3. The universal citizen of the kingdom of Christ believes the gospel, which includes the story of Jesus, especially his atoning death on the cross and his resurrection.

4. The universal citizen of the kingdom of Christ loves God more than anything else. He loves God with all his heart, soul, mind and strength. He also loves Jesus, the gospel and truth. This love motivates him to give his life to the kingdom.

5. The universal citizen of the kingdom of Christ sees himself as a part of a spiritual kingdom, where geography, race, wealth and even history play no part. The establishment of the spiritual kingdom has been God's plan since the foundation of the world, and it fulfills all the promises God has made to human beings. The universal citizen of the kingdom of Christ recognizes Jesus as the king of God's eternal, spiritual kingdom and has no reservations about submitting to Jesus' authority. He also recognizes that the Twelve, as well as other apostles, were inspired by God to continue Jesus' work and to hammer out the details about life in the kingdom. This kingdom is to the universal citizen more

important than food, clothes, even marriage, family and money. The headquarters of this kingdom are in heaven.

6. The universal citizen in the kingdom of Christ seeks to fill his mind with the teachings of Christ. He is careful about his beliefs and teachings so as not to pervert the basic elements of the gospel, such as those just listed.

7. The universal citizen of the kingdom of Christ lives a life of repentance, which means that he is determined to turn away from what is wrong and toward what is good. As one of the basic principles set out in the Beatitudes, he sees the need to grieve over his sins and wants to change.

8. The universal citizen of the kingdom of Christ acknowledges his commitment to obedience. He knows he must live a life worthy of his citizenship in the kingdom. He has no objection to submitting to the authority of God and His Christ. In fact, he acknowledges that his failure to continue to be obedient amounts to a denial of the lordship of Jesus.

9. The universal citizen of the kingdom of Christ pursues righteousness and light and eschews sin and darkness. As one of the basic principles set out in the Beatitudes, hungering and thirsting for righteousness is part of his character.

10. The universal citizen of the kingdom of Christ recognizes that there are greater and lesser commandments and that the greater ones have to do with godly attitudes, such as a concern for suffering people, a general spirit of love for others and a deep trust in God. Though all of God's commandments are important, some are higher and deserving of more attention. As one of the basic principles set out in the Beatitudes, mercifulness, which, according to its meaning in the Old Testament, means serving those who are deprived of the world's goods, must be a major part of his life. The universal citizen of the kingdom of Christ majors in the major things of God's law without ignoring any kingdom principle.

11. The universal citizen of the kingdom of Christ gives special emphasis to Christ-like love. This is the Royal Law. He knows that one of the highest callings of his king is to love others, even as he loves himself.

12. As one of the basic principles set out in the Beatitudes, humility is especially important. In fact, a major aspect of citizenship in the kingdom of Christ is a heart of servanthood, a humble willingness to serve others and not to grasp for power. Servanthood is one of the key profiles of Jesus' kingdom. The kingdom person is also faithful to his personal responsibilities, like the care of his family.

13. As one of the basic principles set out in the Beatitudes, meekness is a part of the disciple's character.

14. The universal citizen of the kingdom of Christ has a willingness to forgive, knowing that he has been forgiven by God through the blood of Jesus. He is especially concerned about his fellow citizens in the kingdom and is willing to forgive them.

15. Because the kingdom is spiritual, the universal citizen of the kingdom of Christ places spirit over flesh, spirituality over sensuality. This is why Paul included the phrase "such things" in his list of the works of the flesh. Jesus also warned people of the seductiveness of money, since it can be a barrier to putting the spirit first. The kingdom person serves God rather than mammon. He seeks to please God rather than men. The universal citizen is very concerned about being enslaved to the flesh. Any behavior that reflects enslavement to the passions of the flesh is sinful.

16. As one of the basic principles set out in the Beatitudes, purity of heart, means having pure motives, thoughts and desires.

17. Also, the citizen of Jesus' kingdom seeks peace. Peacemaking is one of the basic principles of the kingdom, according to Jesus in the Beatitudes.

18. The universal citizen of the kingdom of Christ knows that spiritual growth is essential to his abiding in the kingdom. This growth process would include the following things:

virtue,
knowledge,
self-control,
steadfastness,
godliness,
brotherly love, and
love.

19. As set out in the Beatitudes the universal citizen of the kingdom of Christ is willing to be persecuted for righteousness' sake. He is prepared to suffer with regard to his service to the kingdom and knows that God uses suffering to refine his spirituality. He is committed to conquering these pressures against him. To break under suffering brought on by his commitment to Christ amounts to denying Christ.

20. The universal citizen of the kingdom of Christ produces fruit. His citizenship in the kingdom involves real obedience to the commandments of the king. He also realizes that fruitlessness can result in being expelled from the kingdom. The primary fruits have to do with state of heart, or attitudes. Specifics attitudes would include,

Thankfulness to God for blessings, both physical and spiritual,
joy, that is, a spirit of cheerfulness,
patience,
kindness,
compassion,
goodness,
faithfulness,
gentleness, and
self control.

21. The universal citizen of the kingdom of Christ strives to be transparent. Probably because of the opposition which Jesus faced

from the Pharisees, he made a special point of their externalism, hypocrisy, seeking eminence among men and duplicity.

22. There are things which are prohibited in the kingdom:

having a rebellious, recalcitrant attitude,
arrogance,
duplicity, lying,
omitting those positive traits listed above,
abuse of vulnerable people,
lustfulness or following one's passions,
sexual immorality (which would include things like homosexual behavior, bestiality, incest and probably heterosexual activity outside of the marriage commitment),
idolatry,
adultery,
thievery, stealing, dishonesty, swindling, extortion,
greed, covetousness,
drunkenness,
impurity,
lewdness,
unfitting speech, foolish talk and crude joking, obscenity,
licentiousness,
sorcery,
enmity or malice,
strife,
jealous rivalry,
rage,
selfishness,
stubborn factiousness, or dissension,
slander,
party spirit or divisiveness,
envy,
carousing,
cowardice,
faithlessness,
a rebellious spirit,

a reviling spirit towards things that deserve respect, and murder.

If these behaviors are persistent, and the sinner is continuously impenitent, then he has no place in the kingdom.

23. There are two rituals which are explicitly and essentially connected to the kingdom. One is baptism, which is the immersion in water of a person who accepts the gospel and repents by turning his life over to Christ. This ritual, which Jesus very likely continued to practice throughout his ministry and passed on to his disciples, is the ritual of entrance into the kingdom of Christ. Baptism is so radical that, when properly understood and entered, it constitutes a new birth. The second ritual is the Lord's Supper, which is a ritual that is repeated often, symbolizing one's continued commitment to the gospel. It is characteristically done with other citizens in the kingdom.

24. The universal citizen in the kingdom of Christ recognizes a special responsibility to love other citizens of the kingdom. This especially involves the responsibility to bear the burdens of others in the fellowship. He also recognizes his responsibility to be at peace with his brothers and sisters in the kingdom and to be cheerful and encouraging.

25. The universal citizen in the kingdom of Christ knows that worship does not have to do with certain days and times, but rather worship is the whole life of obedience to the king, twenty-four hours a day, seven days a week.

26. The universal citizen of the kingdom of Christ senses a responsibility to reflect the glory of God to the rest of the world. He knows he has been called to live a life of holiness, that is, a lifestyle which will often be seen as quite different from the way others are living. He must be a light to the world and unashamed to confess his commitment to the lordship of Jesus Christ.

Some Unexpected Absences

The above is what is obligatory on all Christians in every place in every period of time, no matter what the specific cultural conditions might be. But as we stated at the opening of this chapter, not only is it our aim in this chapter to set out a description of the universal citizen of the kingdom of Christ, but we also want to look at some obvious omissions, that is, things which are traditionally considered to be practices, behaviors or doctrines necessary to Christianity, but according to the algorithm are not.

Probably one of the things that is the most conspicuous by its absence would be going to church on Sunday. Not only is that phrase "going to church on Sunday" not even to be found in the Bible, but nowhere is church attendance stated to be an essential aspect of the kingdom. In modern Christianity the things that are done during a corporate assembly have been put in the center of Christian life, as if the Sunday assembly was one of God's main concerns. Now, we did find that loving your spiritual brothers and sisters, encouraging them, and being open to their encouragement are essential aspects of kingdom citizenship, but we found nothing about the necessity of worshiping God in an assembly of Christians on Sunday. So, however disciples of Jesus might decide to encourage their brothers and sisters is up to them in every generation. We're not saying that getting together on Sunday is bad; we're just saying that it's optional.

Church attendance as worshiping God on Sunday is an interesting example because of the way the supposed obligation to do so has been arrived at. The argument goes something like this. The Sabbath is one of the Ten Commandments. Jesus was raised from the dead on Sunday. Christians were urged to assemble (Hebrews 10.25), therefore disciples of Christ today are obligated to observe Sunday as a Christian Sabbath. There is so much wrong with this argument that it is hard to know where to begin. In the Old Testament, it is true, the Jews were commanded to observe the Sabbath day, from sundown on Friday to sundown on Saturday, in honor of the seventh day of creation. But that is just our point: inasmuch as Jesus was raised on Sunday, we would expect to find a clear statement in the New Testament documents enjoining disciples to remember Sunday in honor of Jesus' resurrection, but that we do not find. Next, there is no statement in the New Testament which transfers the Sabbath day to Sunday; neither is its observance attached to the kingdom. In other words, there is no Christian Sabbath. Finally, worship in the New Testament is the Christian life (Romans 12.1-2, 1 Peter 2.4-5). There simply is no depiction of specific acts of worship with are to be done on certain days by Christian disciples. So, this is not only an example of applying things in the Bible to modern Christians which were never meant to be applied, but worse, applying traditions which have grown up over the years.

And it gets even worse. Enjoining Sunday worship actually violates a kingdom principle. As we saw above in Romans 14, the kingdom of God is not about food or drink, or the observance of days, but is rather about righteousness, peace and joy. Similarly, if the example of Christians assembling on the first day of the week (we do find such an example in Acts 20.7) is binding on Christians of all generations, then all the other examples of what the early Christians did, such as raising holy hands and wearing veils, would also be binding on us today. So, it is not just a matter of binding things which are not even mentioned in the Bible, but also a matter of being inconsistent.

In fact, the whole issue of styles of worship activities in the corporate assembly is completely absent from teachings on the kingdom. When we say that such issues are absent, we do not mean to say that it would be wrong for Christians today to assemble on Sundays and engage in various types of activities; we are just saying that such matters are optional. If a certain group of Christian disciples today wish to have certain programs which they believe helps them feel closer to God, that would be their option; but it certainly is not incumbent on Christians in general.

This carries over to other items as well, such as the giving of money. Tithing to the church is not a kingdom requirement. Renouncing all that you have for the sake of the kingdom is a kingdom requirement, but just exactly what that entails is left up to the individual disciple. Similarly, whether an actual church building is erected for mass assemblies is also a matter of option. Loving and serving your Christian brothers and sisters is a kingdom requirement, but disciples in all places and times are free to work that out the way that they believe is best in their circumstances. A certain type of building is not required.

Furthermore, church organization is a matter of option. Probably, very few Christian groups today are organized exactly the way the early church was organized. This is true at least because the early church had apostles; and if we are correct, the apostles were a temporary phenomenon in the history of the church. So, churches could have an elaborate organizational structure, or none at all. Some churches might choose to have a pope, while others might choose to function entirely in terms of autonomous democratic communities. The type of church polity is up to the discretion of various Christian groups. The early church appears to have been organized in terms of the cities in which the Christians lived. A group of men, who were called elders, bishops, pastors, or presbyters, collectively shepherded the Christians in that city. Perhaps the early disciples met in small groups in these elders' homes, but that is not eminently clear. This is the way the first Christians organized themselves, and there is much to be said for the arrangement; but Christians today are not obligated to follow that pattern. The early church also had apostles, who apparently ranged over large districts, but it is not incumbent upon us today to try to imitate that pattern.

In many churches there have been issues surrounding the use of musical instruments. For example, in our own heritage (the authors of this book) there has been a lively debate for decades over the propriety of instrumental music in the Sunday assembly. Some regard it as acceptable, even obligatory, while others regard the practice as outright sinful, endangering the user's salvation. In other religious groups, some instrumentation is allowed, such as harps, pianos, or organs, but others are roundly condemned, such as electric guitars, saxophones and drums. There are even some churches that condemn the singing of any songs other than the Psalms of the Old Testament. The Kingdom Algorithm settles this matter. Not only for the reasons stated above about worship, but nowhere in the Bible is there to be found any statement about kingdom music. Kingdom people today can do anything they wish about music, as long as they don't violate any of the kingdom principles, such as insensitivity to others or self glorification, as listed above.

Before leaving the area of church organization, we should also probably take note of the modern day hot button issue revolving around the role of women in the church. If we are right in our theory of how to apply the Bible to our lives today, then it would appear that whatever roles women might assume today is also up to our discretion. It is possible that, under the rubric of headship, as we saw in Chapter 6, in the kingdom males are to exercise some leadership over females (though it is not very clear), it still remains to be worked out as to what that might mean. Still further, since the assembly is not a kingdom issue, the headship of males wouldn't tell us much about what would be allowable when men and women are together in the assembly. Paul and the other church leaders had to take the principles of Jesus and apply those principles to the churches in their areas of work, and they did so under the inspiration of the Holy Spirit. But it is the principles of the Kingdom which are eternal and universal, not the particular apostolic applications to their situations.

It behooves us at that this point to go back to our fundamental question, that is, how do we apply the Bible to our lives today as Christ followers? We should be reminded that reading the Bible as a manual has proven to be clumsy at best, and inconsistent at worst. As a result, we have proposed another theory of biblical application, that is, that those passages in the Bible which deal with the kingdom are passages that apply to all citizens of Jesus' kingdom for all time. But we also find specific statements about husbands and wives, parents and children, masters and slaves, prayer and other conduct. Are these also kingdom issues? We say no. The specific injunctions of Paul and the early church leaders are examples of how they applied the principles of the kingdom to their situations. We can glean wisdom from their example, but those examples are not binding over the kingdom.

This, once again, raises the distinction between the proper interpretation of a passage and its application. There are passages in the Bible that we might properly interpret and still say that they do not apply to the lives of the disciples in the kingdom at all times and in all places. In the Old Testament, Jewish men under the law were prohibited from trimming the corner of their beards. We might interpret this passage correctly, understand it perfectly and still admit that it does not apply to us today. Though everything in the New Testament can be illustrative, it is the principles that matter forever. So, a kingdom wife should always relate to her husband in terms of kingdom principles; in fact, she is obligated to do so. She might also observe how those principles applied to wives in the first century and therefore choose to follow that pattern, but she is not obligated to do so. Similar things could be said about kingdom husbands. A grown child in the kingdom today might choose to obey his parents, as Paul applied kingdom principles to the grown children in the churches which he ruled in his day. And similar things could be said about kingdom slaves and kingdom masters in certain parts of the world today.

This would also be a good place to take up the issue of women wearing veils in 1 Corinthians 11.2-16. If one reads the Bible as a manual, it would be natural to conclude, according the 1 Corinthians 11, that women in the church should wear head coverings or veils. But the veil question is not a kingdom issue. Paul even says that it is a question of judgment (vs. 13). Some of the women in the church in Corinth were being insubordinate and rebellious, and that is what violated the principles of the kingdom. A Christian woman today might decide to wear a veil when she assembles with the church but violate the principles of the kingdom by having a rebellious heart. There are matters which are conditioned by the culture, for example, conventions of modesty, ways of showing respect, what constitutes wealth, what might be considered offensive, or the proper rules of assembly, but what is eternally applicable in the kingdom of Christ is the attitude of submission to God and love for one's spiritual brothers.

Lest we be misunderstood, and the following point will have to be made several times in this book, the examples we find in the biblical texts are neither irrelevant nor useless. They serve to guide us in our decision making, but they are not binding. We would want to keep in mind at all times the great kingdom principles of love, servanthood, and selflessness when we are trying to decide just exactly how we are going to function as a group of Christians today. Those kingdom principles, or attitudes, are indeed binding, but the exact way they are worked out is not. We might look at the examples that we find in the New Testament and discern a certain wisdom in the way these early Christians did things, but we are not bound by those examples.

Leaving the issue of woman's role for now, we come to another large area of conspicuous absence, and that is the area of doctrine. The history of the Christian church is replete with stories of doctrinal fights. There have been many splits, there have been many doctrinal decisions that were based on politics rather than on the Bible and there have been many major philosophical ideologies which have been imposed upon the faith. For example, Calvinism has had a huge impact upon modern Christianity, with its doctrines of original sin, unconditional election, limited atonement, irresistible grace, and the preservation of the saints (though we recognize these five points have been variously construed). These doctrines are at once held dear by a great many people who are intent on serving Christ and are hated by almost as many who are equally intent on serving the same Christ. We find none of these doctrines as essential to the kingdom. There are beliefs that are essential, such as the belief in the one true God, the God of Abraham, Isaac, and Jacob, Jesus' atoning death, and his resurrection from the dead, but these famous Calvinist doctrines are nowhere tied to the kingdom.

In a similar vein, the role of the Holy Spirit today, especially in the United States, is regarded as a very important doctrine to a large number of disciples, but again, we found no specific pneumatology as necessary to be believed in order for one to be in the kingdom.

In a recent popular work by Mark Driscoll and Gerry Breshears, entitled *Doctrine, What Christians Should Believe,* the authors boldly outlined thirteen doctrines that they believe are incumbent upon Christians for all times and places. Chapter One of their book emphasizes the Trinity as one of those essentials. As they admit, and as every careful student of church history knows, the doctrine of the Trinity is a very convoluted one and got worked out in various ways over the period of the first 400 years of Christianity.[1] In contrast to Driscoll and Breshears, we find no particular doctrine of the Godhead set out as an essential belief for citizens of Jesus' kingdom. Even the issue of the deity of Jesus is not so clear. Well intentioned and well meaning interpreters of those passages having to do with the nature of Christ have landed in different places. We think that citizenship in Jesus' kingdom could admit of a rather wide range of interpretations of that subject, as long as the atonement of Jesus' death, his literal resurrection from the tomb as basis of our hope and Jesus' reign as the Messiah are held.

Many Christians would regard holding a certain view of the Bible as essential to being a Christian. Not only is that conspicuously absent from kingdom talk in the New Testament writings, but it's conspicuously absent in general. When one reads the New Testament

---

1 Driscoll and Brashears, *op. cit.,* pp. 28-30

writings, one becomes immediately aware that the New Testament as an entity did not yet even exist and was at most in an inchoate form. There are religious groups that have suffered turmoil over the issue of biblical inerrancy, and though it is indeed an interesting topic, one's view on inspiration and revelation is not a kingdom issue. Certainly, an awareness of Jesus' role as the final revelation of God to man is essential to the kingdom, but just exactly how the Bible relates to that is not.

In a similar vein, the question of which particular theory of interpretation of the texts is correct is irrelevant to one's modern day citizenship in Jesus' kingdom. For example, some Christians today are insistent on a literal reading of many texts. This results in certain literalistic views about creation, the doctrine of the Fall, Satan and demons, and though these issues are fascinatingly interesting, whether one is a literalist or not is not binding upon Christians today.

And the same thing can be said about eschatological doctrines. The issue of the end of the world is a hot one today. Throughout the centuries, many interpretations of the end of the world have occurred, but nowhere is one's doctrine of the final days attached to salvation or citizenship in the kingdom.

A word of caution here. Again, defining interpretation as the act of determining what a text is saying, and application as the act of determining whether and how to live out a teaching in one's life, we're saying that many of the interpretations which have been so important to so many believers need not be regarded as essential to citizenship in the kingdom and salvation, as many have thought. So, unless belief in a doctrine is explicitly set out in the scriptures as essential to the kingdom, believers should feel free to tolerate in their fellowships wide differences of interpretation of that doctrine. But that doesn't mean that one's interpretation, though tolerated, is not dangerous. It could lead to an incorrect theory of application. Or it could lead to one's violating kingdom principles in another area. Moreover, one might interpret a passage correctly but not live out the principles of the kingdom in his life. Similarly, one's theory of application could, and in fact often does, lead him to put emphasis on the wrong things in the gospel, to the extent that he would ignore the really important matters. And of course, even if The Kingdom Algorithm is correct, as we think it is, one still might misinterpret a kingdom principle, and that's a serious thing. But we do believe that adopting The Kingdom Algorithm would in fact encourage more righteousness in our lives.

What all of this means, though, is that we can hold widely divergent views on issues like evolution, the nature of Jesus, the Holy Spirit, angels, demons and end times and still regard each other as brothers and sisters in Christ. In fact, by following the hermeneutics and theory of biblical application promoted in this book, we believe that more fruitful discussion and debate can be had on these topics than we can have by dividing up our fellowships with each group going to its own corner and talking among its own members.

In this section, we are discussing certain issues which we suspect would come to the minds of the readers rather quickly upon considering our view of the Bible and how to apply it to followers of Christ in all times and places. These issues come to mind because they appear to many Christ followers to be Christian essentials. We have looked at issues revolving around church organization and church activities. We have looked at several doctrines which have been regarded as critically important throughout the centuries. We now want to list some practices which are also conspicuously absent from our picture of the kingdom. First of all, would be certain vices like the smoking of tobacco or the drinking of alcohol. There are kingdom principles such as purity and being a good example that would apply to these issues, but those principles don't necessarily mean that a disciple today could never drink alcohol, use tobacco, or even use certain drugs. The use of these substances would be guided by kingdom principles but not necessarily prohibited. As we saw above, issues revolving around food were important to the early Christians, but Paul made it very plain that the consumption of food was in general a matter of private, individual discretion. As he said, the kingdom is not about regulated food but is about righteousness, peace and joy. Drunkenness and self-indulgence could keep someone out of the kingdom, but as for other aspects of these substances, the individual Christian has to work that out for himself.

Though it might seem quaint to some of our readers, there are churches which in the recent past have made practices such as dancing, movie going, card playing and the use of make up and jewelry, deal breaking issues; those who engage in those activities were regarded as unfaithful Christians. Once again, there are principles which guide these behaviors, principles which are inherent to the kingdom of Christ, but relatively few specific practices, such as fornication, lewdness and the lack of self control, are kingdom issues and are listed as prohibiting one from entering the kingdom.

Strikingly, we find that even such things as the widely rejected practice of polygamy are not explicitly listed as blocking one's entrance into the kingdom of Christ. Not only is polygamy never explicitly prohibited (in fact, it is accepted and regulated in the OT), nowhere is it listed among those things that keep one out of the kingdom of God. In our opinion, Christians of all ages should be prepared to accept some widely divergent cultural practices in the lives of their brothers and sisters in the kingdom. This is especially important with regard to missionary efforts in third world countries. However, it bears repeating that everything a disciple does is controlled by kingdom principles (cf. Colossians 3.17). These principles always take into account one's motive and attitude.

Conclusion

We've tried to set out a comprehensive description of what is necessary to being a Christian for all times, in all places and in all cultures. There is always the possibility we left something out, but we believe this is close. Thankfully, repentance is an ongoing aspect of life in the kingdom, and so is God's forgiveness. The things set out above are our goals, our commitment, and we strive everyday to obey them.

One of the values and benefits of our algorithm for applying the Bible to our lives is that many of these issues which have been proven to be so divisive simply need not be so. Just as with the early disciples we read about in the Bible, there can be a great deal of divergence in the beliefs and practices of modern day disciples. Our algorithm is not only consistent, we believe, but it also promotes much more tolerance and inclusiveness.

9 Objections Considered

When it comes to applying the Bible to our lives, we have proposed the following algorithm for doing so: whatever one finds in the Bible as inextricably essential to the spiritual kingdom of Christ is essential for all Christians for all time. However, we are aware that this will not seem, especially at first, to be either necessary or proper by a great many sincere followers of Christ. We have lightly covered some of the following concerns in our remarks so far, but at this point we would like to take them up more directly, even though that will involve a little bit of repetition. So, in this chapter we will raise what we think would be some common objections to the algorithm of the kingdom. These putative objections come from our own experiences in church life. There are probably some objections that people would raise that we haven't thought of, but we believe that the following objections would be common ones.

Objection #1 – An Algorithm Isn't Necessary

Probably the most common objection would go something like this: we don't need an algorithm; why not just read the Bible, believe it, and do what it says? Of course, that very question is the subject of this book. Our response begins by stating that no one is doing this; it only appears to some people that this is going on. In the first chapter we referred to just a few of those things that Scot McKnight calls "blue parakeets", passages which are on the pages of the scriptures, right alongside other passages, which are urged upon others to obey, but are themselves conveniently passed over, as they should be. Virtually no one carries out capital punishment as it was commanded in the Old Testament. Virtually no one follows the dress code of the Bible or the dietary code. Not all Christians pursue charismatic gifts. In fact, when one compares some of the New Testament commandments with those of the Old Testament, the laws in the Bible appear to be even inconsistent. When Jesus told his disciples to leave their boats with their fathers and follow him, we do not take that as a commandment for us today. The fact of the matter is that everyone who tries to live by the Bible has some sort of system, whether or not they are conscious of it, which guides them in applying the Bible to their lives. In most cases, it is just an unjustified, un-critiqued list of do's and don'ts. No one that we know of just reads the Bible, believes it and does what it says. All of this we brought up in the first chapter.

Objection #2 – Why This Algorithm?

This brings us to the next obvious objection, namely, why this particular algorithm? As we admitted above, one could very well have a consistent system, but it still might not be what God wants of us.

First of all, in response, we would argue that, as we saw in Chapter Three, this kingdom is what Jesus came to establish. It was the main point of his ministry. On almost every page of the gospels Jesus is found explaining the nature of this kingdom. He said it was the reason for which he had come (John 18:33-38). All five of the major discourses, as presented by Matthew the apostle, are built around the concept of the kingdom.

But this objection could be restated as follows, if The Kingdom Algorithm is indeed the method we should use to apply the teachings of the Bible to our lives, then why did Jesus just not lay this paradigm out plainly.

Our answer is that he, in fact, did. The famous Sermon on the Mount itself makes our point; it sets out the principles which people would need to employ in their lives in order to enter the kingdom. We are arguing that Jesus had an algorithm, The Kingdom Algorithm, and that this is what God is after in the lives of all of his followers for all times and in all places and that this algorithm is consistent. What other algorithm could there be?

We should also respond that we have not found another hermeneutic that works. In Chapter Two we looked at putative answers to the problem, but we found none that works. One might argue that salvation is just as central as is the kingdom in Jesus' message, so why not make the salvation statements the algorithm, the canon within the canon? But actually we dealt with that. In Chapter Six we considered the point that there are certain things that are in the kingdom, such as salvation, eternal life and a relationship with God, but even if one were to use salvation as the algorithm, he would wind up in the same place, albeit by a more indirect and circuitous route. It is eventually going to come out the same. And there is a reason for that, namely, that salvation, eternal life, etc. are in the kingdom. We prefer the notion of the Kingdom of God as central, because it is in Christ's kingdom that all of these blessings such as salvation can be found. It is possible, though, that terms such as salvation and eternal life are virtually interchangeable with the concept of the Kingdom of God.

Furthermore, can anyone seriously deny that the mission of Jesus was to set up the eternal spiritual kingdom of God? When God saved the Israelites at the red Sea, Moses was taken over by the Spirit of God and sang of the victory of God over the gods of Egypt (Exodus 15). In his song we come across the first reference to God's kingdom, "The Lord will reign forever and ever" (vs. 18). When the people of Israel demanded of Samuel a king, God said to Samuel, "Hearken to the voice of the people in all that they say to you; for they have not rejected you, but they have rejected me from being king over them" (I Samuel 8.7). Even though some of the kings did a good job, the overall experiment with the kings of Israel and Judah was a dismal disappointment. As we saw in Chapter Three above, John the Baptizer and Jesus brought the kingdom of God back to Israel as a fulfillment of all the promises God had made to them. Jesus' kingdom is, therefore, the fulfillment of the major themes of the Bible.

In that light, let us note that, as many, many Bible readers have pointed out, Christianity is the fulfillment of Judaism in the sense that, even though many of the physical trappings of Judaism, such as circumcision, temple worship, and dietary laws, have been stripped away, the great principles of holy living remain intact. If a Jew in Paul's day were to convert to the way of Christ, there is nothing that he would need to change except for acknowledging that Jesus is both the Messiah and the source of salvation by being baptized into him. All of the great principles of Christian living can be found in the Old Testament. This is made clear, incidentally, in Acts 21, where James, the brother of the Lord, enjoins Paul to show clearly to his fellow Jews that by becoming Christians they did not have to abandon Judaism. This means that the kingdom principles are not only prospective, but also retrospective, that is, we can not only say that the principles were for followers of Jesus, but in them we can also see what God had always been demanding of his people. So, this is a further indication that The Kingdom Algorithm is on the right track.

Objection #3 – How Did People Miss It?

To say that The Kingdom Algorithm is indeed the way we should read and apply the Bible to our lives and that no one appears to be making that point does indeed come across as very pretentious. One might understandably ask how it is that Bible students have missed it. We agree that that question alone is enough to give someone pause, and we have indeed been quite intrigued about it. We understand how easy it is to be mistaken about something, and we're aware that we might have got it wrong. However, the problems with the other approaches to applying the Bible remain.

We propose that what causes people to miss something like this is that they are wearing tinted glasses, that is, they are kept from seeing something because they are looking through a filter. There are two main pairs of tinted glasses that we think people have been wearing. The first is the church. We've been brought up to think about the religion of Jesus Christ in terms of the church, where church is usually understood in terms of what we do in an assembly. As a result, we have had the tendency to read the Bible to answer the question of how to organize a church. We've found answers in the Bible to that question sometimes, even if we had to wrench them out of the scriptures a little bit.

The second most commonly worn pair of tinted glasses would be the Bible. We've also been taught that the Bible is the word of God written to us. Or we've been taught that the Bible is a manual for daily living. As long as one looks at the Bible like that, he will have a tendency to think that all of it has been written to him; there would be no drive to find a canon within the canon.

There are other pairs of tinted glasses, though. One would be (and we might have to coin a term at this point) the glasses of "ahistoricalism", that is, reading the Bible flatly, as some people say,[1] which means that the Bible is read as if history didn't matter, as if it was written to us in our day and time. Reading the Bible like that might cause one to miss the historical development of the kingdom of God, as we set it out in Chapter 3, therefore causing him to miss the significance of the kingdom in Jesus' mission. There are also the tinted glasses the people of Jesus' day wore, namely, militaristic messianism. They couldn't understand Jesus because they expected the Messiah to be like David. Finally, there were the tinted glasses the Pharisees wore. They couldn't accept Jesus' message of the kingdom because they were majoring in the minor things of God's law while ignoring the major.

There probably are other things in our culture that prevent us from seeing things in God's word, but we believe The Algorithm of the Kingdom has been there all along.

Objection #4 – Picking and Choosing

Another objection might go like this, "Aren't you just picking and choosing what you want to believe and practice," or stated otherwise, "Isn't your algorithm just a way of coming out with what you want at the end?" That's a fair objection and one certainly worthy of serious consideration. It seems to be our human nature to find a way to do what we wish to do, and whether the algorithm is adopted or not, this objection should be revisited often. However, our answer to those questions

---

1 Russ Dudrey, "Restorationist Hermeneutics Among the Churches of Christ: Why Are We at an Impasse?" *Restoration Quarterly,* Vol. 30, No. 1, 1988, pp. 17-42, p. 41.

would be no; in fact, that is the very thing we are trying to avoid. It seems that every group has a list of do's and don'ts, as well as a list of acceptable and unacceptable doctrines, but the lists differ from group to group. Moreover, even though with some groups there is indeed an algorithm, with most groups this is not so. Things like tradition, convenience and common sense are usually the deciding factors. Our driving concern, though, is to avoid these confusions. Whatever beliefs and practices we might consider binding should be considered so on the basis of a defensible principle, an algorithm.

We would also respond by reminding our readers that consistency is extremely important. Some Christians, for example, still practice speaking in tongues, even though Paul said that tongue speaking would go away (1 Corinthians 13.8); others ignore the passage about women wearing veils (1 Corinthians 11.2-16), even though that commandment was never said to go away. Inconsistency in applying the Bible can be maddening to some, especially newcomers to the faith. Good hearted followers of Christ often settle in and go about living for God, but in the backs of their minds there is the gnawing awareness of inconsistency (this is sometimes referred to as cognitive dissonance). Our algorithm is driven by consistency. In fact, not to be abrasive, we are concerned that most everybody else, and we too in our pasts, have been guilty of picking and choosing. We hope our intentions were pure, but still we did not have a principle of consistently applying the Bible to our lives. Without meaning to do so, most, if not all of us, have been guilty of picking and choosing. The algorithm is designed to help us avoid just that very error. We do not believe that we are picking and choosing according to some preconceived list, whether consciously or unconsciously; rather we believe we have come up with a system, a key if you will, by which we can consistently and faithfully select those principles, beliefs and practices which God would have us follow today. We have sought to find a principle to guide our beliefs and practices today so that we are not capricious or whimsical. This is not picking and choosing. Consistency has been our litmus test. As we showed in Chapter One, so many fine, sincere, followers of Christ still have systems of application which are inconsistent; they will use a principle to enjoin a certain practice from the Bible, while at the same time ignore another practice which would be equally as much demanded by the same principle. That is inconsistent. Now, we are aware that just because someone has a consistent principle of application, it does not mean it is the right one; but inconsistency definitely means we have the wrong one.

Objection #5 – You Are Taking Away From the Bible

Others might object that the algorithm of the kingdom amounts to a canon within the canon; in fact, vast sections of the Bible become noncompulsory under our method. To this we would reply that that is exactly the case. As we stated under the first objection, everyone does indeed have a canon within the canon, whether they are consciously aware of it or not. Many religious groups' canons of applicability are determined by certain historical theological systems. For example, Calvinism, which is a major ideology of modern Christianity, creates a canon within the canon. Calvinism rejects works as essential in Christianity; that's why water baptism is ruled out by Calvinists as being an essential part of salvation. Our (the authors') own fellowship has a canon within the canon. We were taught that as disciples we can do only what is commanded, or approved by an example or an implication (something that can be inferred) from commandments or examples, as found in the New Testament. However, all one has to do is to go to various church websites and read the doctrinal statements to see that most, if not all, churches have restrictions on the entirety of biblical teaching. Nobody follows the whole Bible. No group of Christians of today is amassing arms to go fight the Amalekites, like the Israelites in Kings Saul's day were commanded to do. Everybody has a canon within the canon. They don't obey the Old Testament sacrificial laws, neither do they leave their boats and their fishing nets with their fathers, as Jesus commanded his disciples to do. Some groups think the silence of the scriptures is prohibitive. Some would draw a contrast between "that was then" and "this is now". Again, one has only to go to a church's website today and read their creeds to see how it is standard practice to have a canon within a canon. As we said above, even Jesus had an algorithm for applying the Old Testament law. Jesus had an algorithm which reduced the Bible of his day to a canon within the canon of the Old Testament. Take for example the Sermon on the Mount (Matthew 5-7). Jesus argued in that very sermon that there are certain principles, often referred to as the Beatitudes, which are at the heart of God's will and are tied to the eternal spiritual kingdom of God. Further still, even though Jesus recognized his obligation to obey the whole of the Law of Moses, the Law itself was a subset of the whole of the Bible of his day. In other words, a faithful Jew was not obligated to obey the whole Bible, just the whole law. Also, there are the several confrontations Jesus had with the Pharisees over things like working on the Sabbath. Jesus was anything but a scofflaw. There was a method to his responses. When he pointed out that even animals were rescued on the Sabbath, that the priests worked on the Sabbath, that plucking grain was not a violation of the Sabbath and that healing someone on the Sabbath was allowable, he was not saying that the Law sometimes did not matter; rather he was saying that the Pharisees had misinterpreted the Law by not recognizing certain priorities of some laws over others. Jesus had an algorithm. Paul also had an algorithm for applying the Law. As the books of Acts, Romans and Galatians make very clear, one of the first critical issues for the early generations of Christ followers was whether the Law of Moses applied to Gentile Christians or not. As we all know, they decided that it did not. So, everyone has some sort of algorithm, inconsistent in the case of many of us, by which they single out those passages which they take as applying to them today. This is exactly the problem that we are trying to solve, namely, which algorithm should we choose in order to be faithful to God today.

But we take the idea of the canon within the canon even more seriously. On September 1, 1816, Alexander Campbell enraged a fair number of hearers when he preached what is now famously referred to as "The Sermon on the Law". In it he argued that Christians are not now, nor ever were, under the Law of Moses. We think he was right. We are not wedded to the ideas of Alexander Campbell, but we mention him to point out that the idea that Christians are under only the teachings of Jesus and the apostles is not a new idea. Our heritage (the authors'), the Restoration Movement, has always had a canon within the canon, namely, the New Testament.

We should ask, though, at this point where the canon came from. Nearly every churchgoer is aware that there is a difference between the Catholic and Protestant Bibles. Some of the earliest New Testament collections had in them books like 1 Clement, the Didache, the Epistle of

Barnabas and the Shepherd of Hermas. As stated above, even the Jews were not under the whole of what we call the Old Testament. They were under the Law, but the rest of the Bible was not the law, rather prophets, psalms, wisdom and other writings. The canon of the Coptic Church has the Book of Enoch in it. As heretical as this might sound, the actual collection of the books of the Bible is a human artifact. When the sixteenth century reformers broke off from the Roman Catholic Church, they found themselves in desperate need for religious guidance now that they had separated themselves from the priests of the Roman Catholic Church; the natural response to that desperation was to turn to the Bible. Interestingly, when Martin Luther translated the Bible into German, he omitted the Book of James, which he found objectionable. At any rate, the move from the authority of the Roman Catholic Church to the Bible led to modern evangelical Christians seeing the Bible as their authority. Certainly, that has not been bad, but there have been some problems, one of which is the problem addressed in this book. But the New Testament is a very conservative collection of early Christian documents, and an excellent collection as well. We are thankful that God has preserved it for us today, but we propose instead to see the Bible as a record of God's work in this world, the final installment of which is the kingdom of Christ. Instead of seeing the Bible as authoritative, we suggest that we see the kingdom teachings of Jesus and the apostles as that part of the Bible which is incumbent on all followers of Christ, everywhere, in all cultures and for all times.

As an instructive comparison, consider The Federalists Papers. Each of the essays in this collection originated as a letter to the editor of a newspaper during the period of the early republic of the United States of America. They were newspaper articles, not statutes in a law book. They were written for the people during that historical period when they were debating acceptance of the Constitution. At some point a collection was made and put into two volumes. One can read them today, knowing that each one was written to support a certain side of the debate and that it was written for publication in a newspaper, but still extract from them the basic principles of the new republic. The New Testament is The Federalist Papers for Christians. Though they were written for various audiences at the time that the Jesus movement was just beginning, we today, as citizens in Jesus' kingdom, can extract from those documents the principles of his kingdom, by which its citizens should live in all ages, in all times and under all circumstances. Just as one might extract the principles of the American Constitution from The Federalist Papers and thereby have a canon within the canon, we should extract the principles of Jesus' kingdom from the New Testament, even though that means those principles would constitute a canon within the canon.

Objection #6 – Subordinating the Bible

Some might see us as abandoning the Bible or that we are making the Bible secondary to the algorithm of the kingdom, if not altogether irrelevant. As one young person said in a Bible class on one occasion, "Aren't we supposed to believe the Bible and do what it says?" Now, what most people mean by questions like this is that they have been taught to accept the Bible and to live by it, but as we showed in Chapter One, that's not done as easily as some would make it sound. Let us just say at this point that we have a great respect, even reverence, for the Bible. The Bible is an extraordinary collection of documents which record God's dealings with human beings at various historical points. From these texts we can learn so much about God and what he has required of people over time. As we find in the texts of the Bible, God dealt with people even before there was a Bible. Moses is widely acknowledged as the first writer chronologically, but even he looks back to deeds done by God in the past. In fact, Moses came along a long time after the covenant with Abraham. So, the text of the Bible begins with Moses' ministry and evolves over time, not with Noah or Abraham. Key players in the development of the Bible, besides Moses, include David, Solomon, Jeremiah, and Ezra, who apparently was the first to make scripture central to the lives of God's people. By the time Jesus arrived, these texts had become quite important in Jewish life. After the deaths of Jesus' apostles, the writings of significant Christians began to be collected, and because the Old Testament was treasured by the early Christians as background for Jesus' work, the Old Testament scrolls were eventually combined with the writings of the early church to become the Bible that we have today. But even then, the Bible was not the center of Christianity, rather it was the teachings of Jesus and the apostles which were passed down from mentor to mentor. In fact, the first person in church history who attempted to solve a theological problem by appealing to scripture was Arius, around 312 AD. The Bible in an extraordinary gift to the human race, but the Bible is not the basis of Christianity. What God did for us through the death of Jesus on the cross and his consequent resurrection from the dead, resulting in the establishment of Christ's kingdom on earth, is the basis of Christianity. The fact is that the Bible is not the basis of God's acts in history; the story of those acts is the basis, no matter how it might have been handed down. The story culminates with the establishment of God's kingdom on earth, and it is this part of the story that is eternal and universal. If anything should be central it is the story of God's work with human beings, His promises, the fulfillment of those promises and how important it is to serve God rather than man, in other words, the kingdom.

We believe The Kingdom Algorithm, which we have outlined in this book, honors the Bible. It takes the Bible very seriously. The Algorithm of the Kingdom accepts the Bible as a heuristic guide in our service to God. Today, it is all we have. We are not interested in quibbling over issues with regard to the preservation of the texts over time, the canon, the transmission of the texts, the translation of them into various languages, the necessity of understanding historical background to interpreting the texts properly, the need for lexicographical work nor the matter of biblical authority. The Bible, in English, for an English speaking Christian, is an invaluable tool for following God. We have no desire to deprecate the Bible. Our interest in the book is in how to use it. So, the Bible is anything but irrelevant, but we need to understand what its proper role is in the church for all times. So let's return to the young Bible class student's question, "Aren't we supposed to believe the Bible and do what it says?" Our answer to the question is, of course, and it is by following The Kingdom Algorithm that one is indeed believing the Bible and doing what it says. We are arguing that the other approaches are incomplete and even sometimes absurd. We want the young student to read the Bible and apply it correctly. We don't want him stoning homosexuals because the Old Testament tells him to do so. We don't want him requiring female believers to wear veils. Neither do we want him to waste his time trying to apply a lot of things to his life that were never intended to be applied. And this is not because we don't respect the Bible; it's because we do.

Objection #7 – Unsettling

Some objections to the algorithm of the kingdom spring from a more practical concern, rather than a logical one. For example, some people might find the Algorithm of the Kingdom to be unsettling; it makes them nervous. They feel as if they are in a free fall; gone are all of the stable structures such as church attendance, the giving of money, and Bible reading. Though getting away from a checklist might feel too loose and unstructured to a great many people, the whole point of Christianity is to avoid a mindless checklist and emphasize instead spiritual principles which guide our lives everyday all day long. The latter is more difficult, but it is also far more spiritually rewarding. Jacob Neusner complains in his *Introduction to Judaism* that many young modern Jews today eschew theology, the Bible, going to temple, the traditional rituals and the commandments and displace them with the concern to support the modern state of Israel in the Middle East. He refers to the movement as American Judaism of Holocaust and Redemption. It is displacement religion, which is when people substitute one area of concern for traditional religion.[2] We suspect that the same sort of thing can be found in Christianity as well. For example, one might displace the restrictive religion of his parents with a concern for saving the whales and old growth forests. It is a human disposition to make for ourselves a convenient checklist with which to displace a deep religion which is subservient to the will of God. And checklist religion can even be worse than that. For some people, a short list of do's and don'ts allows them to ignore egregious evil elsewhere in their lives. As we have all seen, one might go to church, give money to a cause and promote certain doctrines, while at the same time mistreat his wife, defraud his neighbors and be a racist. Checklist religion can serve as a distraction from the central concerns of the kingdom of God. So, though The Kingdom Algorithm might be unsettling, it is the center of God's will. God wants his people to struggle every day to have in their hearts the same values that are in His. These values then guide all the activities of our

---

2 Jacob Neusner, The Way of the Torah, *An Introduction to Judaism,* 7th ed., Belmont, Cal.: Wadsworth/Thompson Learning, 2004, pp.255-265.

lives, including church attendance, serving our neighbors and playing with our kids. That is the essence of the kingdom.

Yet another psychological problem which our readers might have with the The Kingdom Algorithm is that it might shake some very cherished beliefs and practices. As we have pointed out before, many things which have over time become familiar aspects of Christianity are not, according to The Kingdom Algorithm, necessary elements of Christianity, for example, church attendance, a particular type of church government, not smoking, not drinking alcohol, wearing the proper garments, the role of the Holy Spirit, the doctrine of the Trinity, the possibilities of miracles, styles of worship, male/female roles, evolution, war, secular holidays and many, many other issues (we listed over 125 such issues in preparing for this publication). Stated in a light hearted way, an objector might complain that the The Kingdom Algorithm robs him of his favorite doctrine or theological hobby. It should go without saying that we should all be ready to jettison any pet theological perspectives if they turned out to be incorrect. Though it is a common practice, deciding up front what we are going to believe and then setting out to prove it is a mistaken approach.[3]

One of the values of The Kingdom Algorithm is that we start with a principle and then our beliefs and practices follow from that. It is principle driven. In fact, we are open to abandoning The Kingdom Algorithm, if it itself turns out to be mistaken or inconsistent. We can become quite attached to certain doctrines and ways of doing things, but just as we would want other people to rethink certain beliefs and practices, we should be willing to do so ourselves. After all, open mindedness (humility) is itself a kingdom issue. The algorithm makes us rethink everything, and that is good. We must resist the urge to entrench ourselves in our beliefs. The proper way to interpret and apply scripture comes first before our beliefs and practices. In fact, the very common tendency to hold on to our traditions has too often affected our way of

---

3 Leading American social psychologists, Carol Tavris and Elliot Aronson, recently wrote about the dangers of incremental self-justification, whereby people slowly, step by step, justify their misdeeds, rather than admit and change them, and over time reach deep levels of depravity. If we start with defending our current position and seek a way to justify it, post hoc, it can lead almost anywhere. See their *Mistakes Were Made (but not by me). Why We Justify Foolish Beliefs, Bad Decisions, and Hurtful Acts*, New York. Houghton Mifflin Harcourt publishing Company, 2007.

approaching the Bible. If we are honest enough to ask ourselves from time to time just how we arrived at the views we have, we can discover inconsistency, or worse, no system of interpretation at all. Sometimes we simply adopt a laundry list of views and hold on to it. Sometimes we try to live with inconsistency (cognitive dissonance, again). And as we said, sometimes the traditional views determine the hermeneutic. But we need to have a consistent system in approaching the Bible first and then allow that system to work, no matter where the process might lead --and yes, even if that leads us eventually to abandoning the algorithm itself.

Objection #8 – Too Nebulous

There is also the matter of spirituality. The concept of a spiritual kingdom is difficult to understand, and that might create a problem for some. Going to church and engaging in rituals would seem to many people to be more intelligible than a nebulous spiritual kingdom. It is basic human nature to be able to deal better with physical things than with the spiritual. Currently in American religion of all sorts, as with Neusner's example of current Judaism, especially among the younger crowd in America, there is much more interest in serving food in a soup kitchen or helping with suffering children than there is with changing one's attitudes. Active serving is certainly good; but there is a human tendency to displace moral development with physical involvement, and that is not good. On the worst level, people will sometimes pick several activities, such as church attendance and the giving of money, charitable activities or several doctrines, and rely on them for their relationships with God, while harboring terribly sinful attitudes, such as envy, hatred, elitism or greed. Dealing with the heart has always been one of the challenging aspects of the one true God. The prophet Samuel told King Saul that no amount of ritual sacrifice can displace an obedient heart (1 Samuel 15.22-24). The eighth century prophets emphasized the point that humility, concern for others and an attitude of trusting in God were more important than any kinds of rituals, no matter how sensational (Isaiah 57.15, Hosea 6.6, 12.6, Amos 5.21-24 and Micah 6.6-8). Jeremiah castigated his fellow Jews for relying on temple ritual to justify them before God while at the same time mistreating their neighbors (Jeremiah 7.1-15). And, of course, this was Jesus' point about the kingdom: guarding our hearts is difficult. Furthermore, by spiritual we do not mean murky, mysterious or mystical. The spiritual kingdom of God is straightforward enough; it just requires constant attention and self-examination.

Objection #9 – Too Rational

Finally, this approach to Christianity might come across as too rational, perhaps too mechanical. There might also be the concern that we have interjected human philosophy, about which Christians in the Bible were warned (eg., Colossians 2.8). There is also the concern that The Algorithm of the Kingdom succeeds only in constructing another "Checklist Christianity", wherein one's relationship with God is understood as ticking off certain selected actions, usually overt, observable behaviors. This is similar to the Objection #3 about picking and choosing.

We agree that there is a certain mechanical aspect to the algorithm. Certainly, as one reads the narrative of God's acts in history, there are principles which seem to emerge. By reading the story one gets to know God, so to speak. And something can be lost by a mechanical approach. Mechanical approaches have sometimes been used to bypass important states of heart, very much like applying civil law. But, of course, The Kingdom Algorithm is mainly about the heart; and though anything can be abused, at least this algorithm emphasizes proper attitudes. We would also return to the points made in Chapter Two; if there are no principles for applying the teachings of the texts of the Bible to our lives, then the whole thing becomes quite subjective. That is the extreme on the other end of the spectrum. Furthermore, there is so much to be gained by having the algorithm. So much has been lost by endless arguments about how to apply certain passages. So many strange applications have been made. More importantly, we are trying to approach the Bible simply. With the The Kingdom Algorithm in mind, even a neophyte can approach the Bible meaningfully and practically and immediately get much out of it, without having to make it all apply. As for the taint of human philosophy, that worry cannot be avoided. Everything is supported by philosophical underpinnings, and we are fair warned about the dangers. But every hermeneutic that everyone has is a philosophical position. Even if one were actually to try to read the Bible and apply every sentence to his own life, that itself is a philosophical view about how to approach the Bible, one, in fact, he will not find in the Bible itself. Probably, what Paul was concerned about in the Book of Colossians was that people should be careful that human traditions not trump the word of God, and that is certainly an important thing.

As for the checklist worry, checklists can be bad, or they can be good. It would certainly be a bad thing for one to choose a list of comfortable behaviors from out of the whole set of Jesus' teachings and make them the center of his spiritual life, basing that list on something other than a sincere desire to be righteous, as we discussed above. And The Kingdom Algorithm does produce a checklist, as we saw. But what if the checklist is God's checklist, the checklist of the kingdom, a checklist of states of heart as well as behaviors, and a checklist which is based on sincerely trying to find what God wants us to be? That would be a good checklist.

We believe that God has spoken to the world. We have no desire to distort that message with human thinking. Rather our whole concern with the algorithm is to honor God and His word by finding a way to apply it to our lives faithfully.

Conclusion

We offer our algorithm as a solution to the problem of how to use the Bible in the 21st century as followers of Christ. We set out the problem to begin with that sincere and devoted people have chosen certain passages and ignored others, but without knowing why they do so, that is, without having an algorithm to guide that selection and de-selection. In Chapters 3-7 we set out our algorithm: whatever is essential to the eternal spiritual kingdom of Christ is essential to all followers of Christ for all time and in all places; otherwise not. After summarizing the results, we attempted to address putative objections to the algorithm. We believe that we have addressed these objections successfully. So, what does this all mean?

First of all, and we should go ahead and get this out of the way, if one accepts The Kingdom Algorithm, it will radically change the way she reads the Bible. Since the Reformation, there has arisen a view of the Bible as the very word of God. This was a natural human development, given the break from the Roman Catholic Church and the consequent need for a foundation for Christianity. But over time, the view took on quite a complicated form. The idea of the Bible as the very word of God includes most of the following. It is usually taken that it is written to the reader, whoever she might be, in whatever period of time. Consequently, everything in the Bible would have to apply to each reader, including the gifts of the Spirit, end times teachings, Jesus' instructions to his immediate disciples, etc. The Bible as the word of God would also imply that the Bible can mean something beyond authorial intent, especially since the identity of the human author, on this view, becomes more or less irrelevant. In this same vein, this view of the Bible would discourage the historical aspect, including the need to do any historical-critical analysis or to see Jesus in his historical context. Bibliolatry becomes a problem, with reading it becoming more of a holy exercise, discouraging using the same rational approach that one would use in reading almost any other book. On this view, the issue of the canon becomes all-important. There has to be a closed canon, which God providentially determined, so that the Bible would therefore become a special holy book. This would also provide for people to become experts on the Bible without having to know outside matters, such as historical backgrounds, literary forms or maybe even biblical languages. And usually, conjoined with this view of the Bible is something like a mechanical view of inspiration and a concomitant view of inerrancy.

This is a big subject, but we will mention it here because of its connection with The Kingdom Algorithm. The things described above are problematic notions. Not only is this not the view of their writings which the original writers had, but the writings often indicate who the recipients were. Therefore, immediately one should realize that there will be things in the text that applied only to them. Also, we should read the Bible the same way we would read any other collection of historical documents. The intent of the human author becomes very important to getting the meaning of the text, and there is no reason to think that the author meant more than he was saying. History becomes very important, as the writings often indicate by making historical allusions. So also do linguistic issues matter. But issues like the mechanical view of inspiration and inerrancy become irrelevant. All of these things fit nicely with The Kingdom Algorithm, but that would be the subject of another book.

Secondly, we should embrace the idea that with regard to the Bible, it is a good thing to have a canon within the canon. Everything in the Bible is important, but not everything in it is directly applicable to us followers of Christ today. That's not because times have changed, making certain things in the Bible passé. It's because God spoke to people at various times and in various ways in order to bring His plan to its final state, namely the spiritual kingdom of Christ, and that the principles of that kingdom comprise the universal aspects of the Bible. Most Christians are happy to accept the Bible as a standard for living (and certainly, we are), though there is wide disagreement as to how to go about doing that. Hence, this book. Christians seem reticent, though, to accept the fact that it is a good thing to select certain passages, while ignoring others. We need to get over that. Some Christians are aware that the Old Testament, though extremely useful and extraordinarily enlightening, is not binding on followers of Jesus. The Old Testament, though a major part of the Bible, is not directly applicable to us. The great story that unfolds in the Old Testament lays the groundwork for Christ, and so much of the New Testament is hard to understand very well without a knowledge and appreciation of the Old. Yet, the commandments of the Old Testament are not binding on us Christians. And as we showed earlier, there are many passages in the New Testament that don't apply to us today either. For example, Jesus said many things to his train of immediate disciples that would not apply to us today. And writers such as Paul had specific instructions for his followers that would not apply to us today. The New Testament is a collection of extremely important documents put together by the early church. In this collection there are biographies of Jesus, followed by a story of the first thirty or so years of the apostles' work. There are also letters from various important figures to certain Christian groups, and there is an apocalyptic work which was originally preached to Christians in ancient Turkey to encourage them in the coming difficult days. But not all of the New Testament is directly applicable to us. It's even addressed to specific people, and their specific problems and circumstances are mentioned by the writers. However, from this wonderful collection of early writings we can extract the principles of Jesus' spiritual kingdom, and our first duty should be to read the Bible to find the kingdom. Again, some readers of the Bible understand this. It is also true of us all that we have for all our lives operated with a canon within the canon. The problem has been that we have not been aware of how we have obtained that narrower canon. We have felt uneasy about this practice, but in this book we are suggesting that we should not feel uneasy about it but rather acknowledge the necessity of reducing binding biblical teachings to that narrower group of those things that Jesus intended to be followed by all of his followers throughout the ages. It is very much like using the English language. Native English speakers are often unable to explain to their foreign friends why a certain usage is incorrect or why American English speakers say things the way they do. In our minds, there is the gnawing suspicion that there is a rule that makes one linguistic usage correct and another usage incorrect, but we are unable to enunciate that rule. What we have attempted to do in this book is to enunciate a principle, a principle that can be rationally defended, which sets out clearly what teachings of the Bible are binding upon us today as citizens of the kingdom of Christ.

So, how do we read the Bible and apply it to our lives today? First, all of the well known hermeneutical principles still apply. It remains important to respect the various contexts of the biblical literature just as we do when we read other literature. There is also the issue of translating the original Hebrew and Greek texts into the vernacular, and that work still has to be done. Then, when one reads the text in a modern language, one needs to continue to be concerned about the historical context, that is, who the writer was, to whom was he writing, what the issues were that confronted the writer and his audience, as well as what cultural conditions might enlighten the text. Then there are such matters as literary style: is the text a poem, a letter, a treatise, or even such a thing as an apocalyptic writing? Style always affects the meaning of the text. Lastly, there is the textual context. Just as you and I dislike our sentences being taken out of context, so also should we respect the writers' contexts in the Bible. It remains important to read the paragraphs before and after the particular passage in question. It is also important to read other writings by the same author to see what he said about similar subjects. And finally, there is the context which emerges from all Christian writers who wrote on a particular subject. But this is nothing new. Any reader of any piece of literature always has to deal with these things.

Furthermore, and this point ought to be emphasized more often than it is, the Bible reader ought to read from the bottom up rather than from the top down. Let us explain that. To read a text from the top down is to already have decided what the text is supposed to say and then to read the text to support those preconceived conclusions. For example, some people believe in the doctrine of original sin, and others do not. But let us take, for example, a person who believes in original sin, when she approaches the Biblical text, she might be disposed to read any text she comes across as supporting the doctrine of original sin, even in many cases where the passage has nothing to say about that issue; but if she already believes that that is what the Bible is supposed to say, she will have a tendency to find those teachings in the text. It's very much like giving a boy a hammer; very soon everything looks like a nail to him. But we propose reading the Bible from the bottom up, that is, to make a strenuous effort to let the biblical writer say what he meant to say to his audience in his own context. Then after collecting all of such statements on any topic, the interpreter attempts to organize and systematize those ideas. In other words, one's doctrine emerges from the text rather than using the text to support what we already believed it said. The top down approach to reading the Bible has also been referred to as proof texting. We are opposed to proof texting, as are many other students of the Bible. However, again, this is nothing new. Many would encourage this honest, bottom up approach to reading the Bible. Our concern in this book, though, has been to determine what to do with the Bible even after it has been properly interpreted.

The Kingdom Algorithm says that, as we study the scriptures, we try to isolate those principles, practices and doctrines which are essential to the kingdom and that those, and only those, are binding upon Christ followers for all times, cultures and geographical districts. That has been our only concern in this book, namely, to determine what is the eternal and universal nature of Jesus' movement. Though everything in the Bible is illustrative, we do not want to get bogged down trying to replicate things that were part of the culture of the biblical writers and not meant to be a part of Christians' lives for all times. Let's rehearse briefly, as we conclude, what kingdom living is. The universal citizen in the Jesus' spiritual kingdom knows who God is and what He did for human beings through the ministry of Jesus. As a result, he makes the commitment to turn away from sin and to pursue righteousness for the rest of his life. Upon making this commitment formal by being baptized, he gives an emphatic place to those commandments of

Jesus which rule one's heart, such as the Beatitudes, but he also realizes that, since the kingdom is spiritual, he needs to emphasize spirit over flesh, persistently concentrating on producing the fruits of the spirit and avoiding the works of the flesh. Finally, he is dedicated to serving his Christian brothers and sisters, as well as serving others.

Kingdom living is mainly about motive. Most human problems result from bad attitudes. Arrogance, for example, is a very common bad attitude. A person can have a heart which is unteachable, unwilling to change or resistant to the rules; no real spiritual growth can occur as long as this arrogance remains. Having a humble, pliable and submissive heart is, in fact, more valuable to God than getting things right otherwise. In other words, a disciple might have a good heart and still get some doctrine wrong. He might sin through inadvertence, ignorance or weakness, but he still tries to get back on track and do things right. This God loves more than the person who might do certain things right but has a bad attitude. People can go to church for all the wrong reasons. A person might get dipped in the water but not commit himself to a life of discipleship. He might be a part of worship team but not really be about praising God. He might go through the ritual of the Lord's Supper but not love and serve his brother. He might follow the rules about divorce and remarriage but never had loved his mate sacrificially. God knows our hearts and knows why we do the things we do.

Our concern has been to come up with and to defend a process by which we can find out from the Bible what God intends for the lives of His people in all ages and circumstances. Yet, after we have garnered the teachings about the spiritual kingdom, which are directly applicable to our lives today, there is still so much we can do with the Bible. We need to know the narrative. From one story after another we see certain principles emerge, and most, if not all, of the principles will be reiterated in Jesus' kingdom. But it is so valuable to see these principles evinced in the stories of the Bible. There is a certain power in seeing the principles lived out. As all Bible readers are aware, the aspects of human nature are much the same from time period to time period. The stories caution us about things in our own lives. We see God repeatedly starting over with failed human beings. His love for human beings is so remarkable and so encouraging that it transports us to a higher plain of noble service. The story swells to a crescendo in the ministry, death and resurrection of Jesus of Nazareth, and we can gain a great deal of motivation from seeing ourselves as a part of that continuing story.

There is also the wisdom aspect of the scriptures. Not everything has to be a commandment. We see this is the Wisdom Literature of the Old Testament, especially. The Book of Psalms is not about commandments, though the psalmists often extolled the value of obeying the commandments of the Lord. But the main point is the glorification of God. There are also the psalms of thanksgiving, confession of sin, crying out to God for deliverance, longing for God and even psalms which ask why. These are not collections of commandments, but they do inspire our souls and cause us to look more closely at our lives before God. Very much the same could be said about Proverbs, Job, Ecclesiastes and the Song of Solomon. It is also the same with the New Testament. Who has not sympathized with the disciples as they struggled to understand the nature of Jesus' mission? Paul's problems with the churches ring familiar bells with us in our struggles to serve in the churches. And the Book of James is a New Testament book of proverbs. There is much wisdom to be found in the writings of the New Testament. We do not today have to organize our congregations the same way the early churches did, but it might be wise to do so. We do not have to have house churches the way they did, but it might be wise to. We do not have to tithe, but we might want to give more. Even the instructions to masters and slaves could be instructive to us today. We have not sought to free people from commandments. We actually had no doctrinal agenda at all. Our only concern was to have a well-supported and consistent way of applying the Bible to our lives. In fact, a desire to wriggle free from God's commandments is hardly hungering and thirsting for righteousness. But the point is that, though we are not bound to New Testament commandments which were an application of kingdom principles to the circumstances of the first believers, we should be anxious to find as much wisdom and guidance in those instructions as might be there to find.

It is because of the nature of the kingdom that we espouse The Kingdom Algorithm. It is not because the algorithm solves problems; however, it does solve problems. So many doctrinal problems become irrelevant, as far as fellowship is concerned. Issues like the Trinity, evolution, the work of the Holy Spirit, the possibility of miracles, original sin, Satan and demons, the inerrancy of scripture, heaven, hell and eschatology need not divide brothers. These issues will forever be of great interest to many followers of Christ, but they cease to be central. In fact, we need to cultivate an atmosphere where these issues can be openly debated, each side being heard, and people left with the freedom to decide for themselves. Furthermore, issues about church life can be handled similarly. Issues like church government, the church name, activities done in the assembly, instrumental music, preachers, buildings and programs, again, need not divide us. Similarly, there will be individual differences with regard to how to apply the principles of the kingdom. People will come down in different places on issues like apparel, smoking tobacco, drinking alcohol, diet, going to war, participating in government, money, physical fitness, entertainment and educating children. Sincere people might decide differently on these matters. Instead of isolating ourselves from our brothers and sisters who differ with us, we need to be around Christians who think differently than we do. In fact, there's the possibility that we might change our minds; there's also the possibility they might change theirs. And then there's the possibility that we might learn better how to accept others with different points of view (this sounds a lot like Romans 14, doesn't it?).

We need also to confess that we realize that The Kingdom Algorithm will not solve every problem. There will always be difficult issues, like the war question. Life is complicated, and many tensions can compete in our decision making. However, the algorithm will lead us to the right principles to apply.

One implication of The Kingdom Algorithm is that patternism has to go. Patternism is the view that says we moderns should still try to imitate the early disciples – in every way. That means that we should organize churches the same way they did, have assemblies the same way they did, do mission work the same, etc. In our fellowship, patternism was expressly enjoined. But it never worked. It couldn't. The apostles are gone, the miracles appear to have ceased and many other things that applied to them do not have application to us. One thing that isn't gone, though, is the kingdom of Christ, with its eternal principles and practices.

This brings us to another important issue, perhaps the most important issue in this book. Our algorithm is inclusive rather than exclusive. The Kingdom Algorithm invites unity, rather than inciting division. These central aspects of the kingdom of Christ are things around which people can unite, while at the same time disagreeing on a wide range of beliefs and practices. This algorithm encourages mutual respect and acceptance. It teaches us how to engage in meaningful dialogue with one another, while maintaining a close fellowship built upon a core of kingdom teachings. It takes away that pressure which comes from a sense of obligation to obey everything which the Bible says. The Bible ceases to be a handbook for church life and Christian living and becomes instead a collection of venerable documents from which we can extract the essence of what God requires of his people. This means that we can have unity while at the same time listening to one another, disagreeing with one another, and engaging in dialogue with one another over those disagreements.

None of this is to say that anything goes in Christ's kingdom, which it might sound like to some hearers. The kingdom principles are the kingdom principles. The things we set out for the universal citizen of the kingdom of Christ are not to be compromised. This, of course, is not to say that we couldn't have gotten some of the items wrong. Nor can we be sure that we covered every point. This is a work in progress. Discipleship is a work in progress. But we do think that The Kingdom Algorithm is what God would have us use in applying His principles to our lives. Alas, different groups might indeed decide that the line should be drawn elsewhere, leading to a separation between Christ believers. Given human nature, the algorithm itself, if implemented, will probably be abused. We are not so naïve as to think that those things will go away. However, our contribution to the question of how to approach the Bible is what we have outlined above, and at least it is a system. We think it is consistent, comprehensive and simple. We also think it is at the heart of God's will for human beings.

We wish now to close this chapter with a discussion of two more concerns. As we just said, we suspect that The Kingdom Algorithm could still be abused, even if accepted; just about anything can be abused. So, the first of these concerns is to project into the future how this might happen. In fact, we worry that the algorithm might be abused in such a way as to distort the very purpose for which it was created. In the history of Christianity many things have started off with good intentions only to become sources of falsity and abuse later on. In the Middle Ages leaders in the church were concerned about true repentance. Christians had buckled under the pressures of persecution and temptation. Later, some of these lapsed Christians wanted to come back to the faith, but the question of their sincerity was raised. There were those who wondered if the church was simply being too easy on these returnees. The early Christian leaders Cyprian and Novatian thought that certain standards ought to be set up so that these people could prove their sincerity. But later, in spite of the original intentions of those leaders, these standards turned in the doctrine of penance, a doctrine which taught that sins needed to be paid for by certain rigorous activities, such as fasting, pilgrimages and acts of service; and even later this false doctrine of penance turned into the infamous practice of selling indulgences, whereby certain people paid for their sins with money. Our point is that a method might begin with the best of intentions and later turn into egregiously abusive practices. This raises the question of how The Kingdom Algorithm itself might be so abused.

One possible future abuse which comes to mind immediately is that one might want to say that since the kingdom of God is mainly about attitudes, then as long as one has sweet intentions it would not matter what his behaviors were. For example, since we are to love one another, even a homosexual lifestyle might be acceptable as long as one's motives were sweet and sincere. But we would respond that, as we saw in the above examination of the kingdom, fornication, which includes homosexual behavior, is incongruent with the nature of the kingdom. Paul, for example, explicitly names fornication as an activity which would exclude someone from the kingdom. Or, someone might conclude, falsely, from The Kingdom Algorithm that since there is no Christian Sabbath he doesn't need to associate with and serve his fellow kingdom citizens. But that would, in fact, violate the principles of the kingdom. There are commandments in the kingdom, and we citizens need to be serious about keeping all of those commandments. Just as we have been told by our teachers that we cannot pick and choose from the Bible which commandments we will obey and which we will not, neither can we pick and choose from the principles, doctrines and practices of kingdom which ones we will accept and which ones we will not.

Another possible abuse would be the famous one of starting with a belief or practice and then finding a way to force it to fit the algorithm whether or not it really does. Sometimes people have things that they wish to enjoin or proscribe and they find them in the Bible even though they are not really there. Similarly, one might do the same with The Kingdom Algorithm. It might seem strange that we would suggest that such could happen, but over the centuries, people have proven themselves to be quite ingenious at making things come out the way they want them to come out. This is one of the main reasons we have presented the algorithm the way we have. We are actually insistent that explicit kingdom passages be made obligatory, and only them. We are including the alternate kingdom words and the salvation terms, but it should be incumbent on someone to show that there is an explicit statement in the text to the effect that a certain belief, principle or practice is essential to citizenship in the kingdom, or submission to the authority of Christ or salvation (along with the cognates for these things) before he be able to say that those beliefs, principles or practices are obligatory. We believe that the power of any hermeneutical principle lies with starting with the principle and not where we want it to end up. However, the very intention of seeking an algorithm in the first place was to militate against this kind of hermeneutical abuse.

In a similar vein, we need to note that any system can be twisted. One can make another person say anything they want them to say, if they try hard enough. We recognize that there might be those in the future who would have us implying certain beliefs and practices which are not at all what we are trying to say. So, we recognize that this approach can be twisted to mean things that we never meant to say and we warn against that abuse even now.

Sometimes the Bible has been used to abuse other people. In Paul's day, brothers in Christ sometimes abused each other with their freedoms. Even though they were free to engage in certain activities, they were insensitive to where other people were in their Christian walk see 1 Corinthians 8). We have no doubt that this could be done with our method as well. Of course, being insensitive to other people, especially to our brothers and sisters in Christ, is diametrically opposed to the nature of the kingdom, but that very fact might not keep users of the algorithm from doing that very thing.

Finally, we can think of this possible abuse. Sometimes people become so wedded to their approach to the Bible that they refuse to see the problems inherent in their approach. We recognize our fallibility. We understand that this approach to reading and applying the Bible could be mistaken, and may God help us not to be so in love with our ideas about how to apply the teachings of Christ that we stubbornly hold onto those ideas even in the face of obvious inconsistencies.

We all know something about human nature. The Bible tells us a lot about human nature, and so does church history. The human disposition is to fossilize. This book is a living attempt to derive a method of how to read and apply the Bible to life in all times and places. The method must stay alive. The method has to do with using an algorithm to derive, in a recursive way, answers to our questions about Christian living in whatever age we find ourselves. If this book were to become someone's Bible, then our efforts have failed. What we mean by this is that we recognize that the potential is there for someone to itemize certain aspects from this book, this treatment of the kingdom, and then to take that itemized list as their religious code, while forgetting how the list was derived. We offer this algorithm as a method instead of a list. We are under no illusions that every single question has been answered. Surely the things we have seen in this book will be improved upon in the future, but we believe that the method is eternal. As we said in Chapter Two, everyone has a method of applying the Bible to his life, and there have been many algorithms throughout the centuries, but we offer this one as one which avoids the problems of the previous ones and can be consistently applied from generation to generation. As far as this book goes, it's the algorithm that counts, not the particular list of principles and actions which we have outlined in this book. And this is only because it is the kingdom that counts.

In closing let us say again that, as with everything else, we could be wrong about this. Let us also say that other approaches to the scripture, as we showed above, have not proven to be successful. So this is our best approach to date for dealing with the question about how to use the Bible to direct our lives today as modern citizens of Christ kingdom. But if we are mistaken, we hope we are mistaken on matters of lesser importance. It is clear to us that the kingdom that God established through Christ was meant to be eternal and was at the heart of Jesus' teaching. May our humble efforts somehow serve to promote that kingdom.

Made in the USA
San Bernardino, CA
06 June 2017